Science

Arctic Fox

Harcourt
SCHOOL PUBLISHERS

Orlando   Austin   New York   San Diego   Toronto   London

Visit *The Learning Site!*
www.harcourtschool.com

Arctic Fox

HABITAT Arctic foxes live on the coast and islands of the Arctic Ocean. They live in burrows dug in the side of hills or cliffs.

CHARACTERISTICS The arctic fox uses its bushy tail to stay warm.

Atlantic Ocean

Pacific Ocean

Pacific Ocean

Indian Ocean

SELF-PROTECTION A small nose helps the arctic fox live in cold climates.

CAMOUFLAGE In the summer, the fur is short. It is brown, gray, or blue.

Consulting Authors

Michael J. Bell
Assistant Professor of Early Childhood Education
College of Education
West Chester University of Pennsylvania

Michael A. DiSpezio
Curriculum Architect
JASON Academy
Cape Cod, Massachusetts

Marjorie Frank
Former Adjunct, Science Education
Hunter College
New York, New York

Gerald H. Krockover
Professor of Earth and Atmospheric Science Education
Purdue University
West Lafayette, Indiana

Joyce C. McLeod
Adjunct Professor
Rollins College
Winter Park, Florida

Barbara ten Brink
Science Specialist
Austin Independent School District
Austin, Texas

Carol J. Valenta
Senior Vice President
St. Louis Science Center
St. Louis, Missouri

Barry A. Van Deman
President and CEO
Museum of Life and Science
Durham, North Carolina

Ohio Reviewers and Consultants

Linda Bierkortte
Teacher
Parkmoor Urban Academy
Columbus, Ohio

Napoleon Adebola Bryant, Jr.
Professor Emeritus of Education
Xavier University
Cincinnati, Ohio

Laurie Enia Godfrey
Director of Curriculum Development
Lorain City Schools
Lorain, Ohio

Christine Hamilton
Curriculum Specialist
Toledo Public Schools
Toledo, Ohio

Jerome Mescher
Science/Math Coordinator
Hilliard City Schools
Hilliard, Ohio

Cheryl Pilatowski
Science Support Teacher/Coordinator
Toledo Public Schools
Toledo, Ohio

Lisa Seiberling
Elementary Science Coordinator
Columbus Public Schools
Columbus, Ohio

Kathy Sparrow
Science Learning Specialist, K–12
Akron Public Schools
Akron, Ohio

Matthew Alan Teare
Science Resource Teacher
Miles Park Elementary School
Cleveland Municipal School District
Cleveland, Ohio

Shirley Welshans
Teacher
Parkmoor Urban Academy
Columbus, Ohio

EARTH AND SPACE SCIENCES

Science Spin
Weekly Reader

Technology
Be Earth's Friend, 50

People
Studying Rivers, 52

LIFE SCIENCES

Science Spin
Weekly Reader

Technology
Traveling Turtles, 86

People
Feeding Time, 88

PHYSICAL SCIENCES

OHIO EXPEDITIONS

Your Guide to Science in Ohio

Ready, Set, Science!

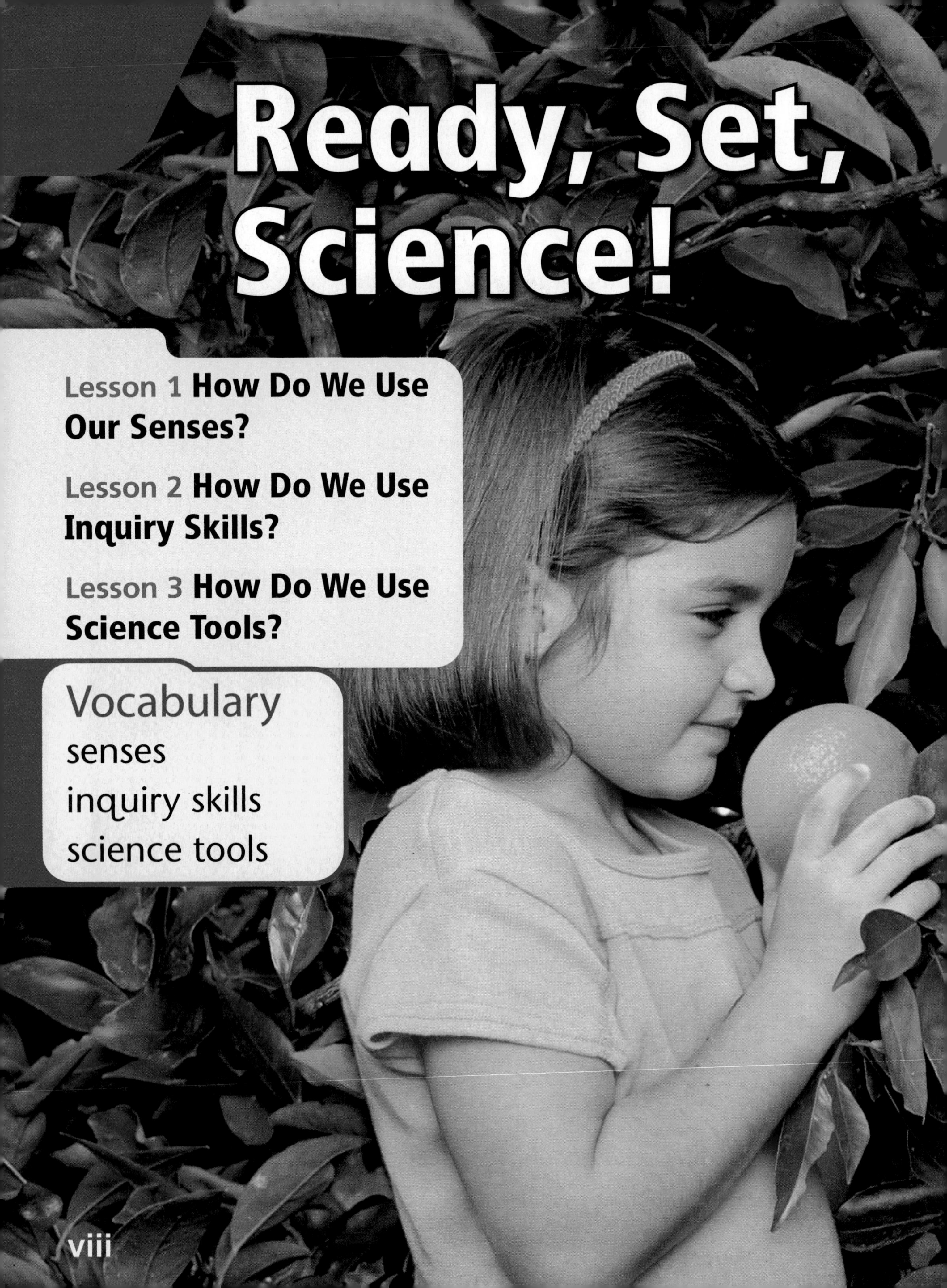

Vocabulary
senses
inquiry skills
science tools

I wonder...

Can kids be scientists?

What do **YOU** wonder?

How Do We Use Our Senses?

Fast Fact

You have about 10,000 taste buds on your tongue! You can use taste and other senses to predict things.

How Your Senses Work

You need

- oranges
- bananas
- apples

Step 1

Close your eyes. Your partner will give you a piece of fruit.

Step 2

Smell the fruit. Then taste it. **Predict** which kind of fruit you will see when you open your eyes. Was your **prediction** correct?

Step 3

Trade places with your partner. Repeat.

Inquiry Skill

When you **predict**, you tell what you think will happen.

SI-1 Infer/Predict, **SK-1** Discover that experiments are repeatable   **3**

VOCABULARY
senses

 READING FOCUS SKILL

MAIN IDEA AND DETAILS Look for details about using senses.

Your Senses

People have five senses. The five **senses** are sight, hearing, smell, taste, and touch. You use different body parts for different senses.

MAIN IDEA AND DETAILS
What are the five senses?

touch

hear

see

smell

taste

4

Senses Help You

Your senses help you observe and learn about many things.

MAIN IDEA AND DETAILS
How can your senses help you learn?

5

Using Senses Safely

Keep your body safe. Use safety equipment when you need to. Follow these safety rules.

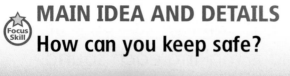

MAIN IDEA AND DETAILS

How can you keep safe?

Wear gloves.
Wear goggles.
Wear an apron.
Don't touch anything hot.
Don't put anything in your mouth unless your teacher tells you to.

Focus Skill **1. MAIN IDEA AND DETAILS** Copy and complete this chart.

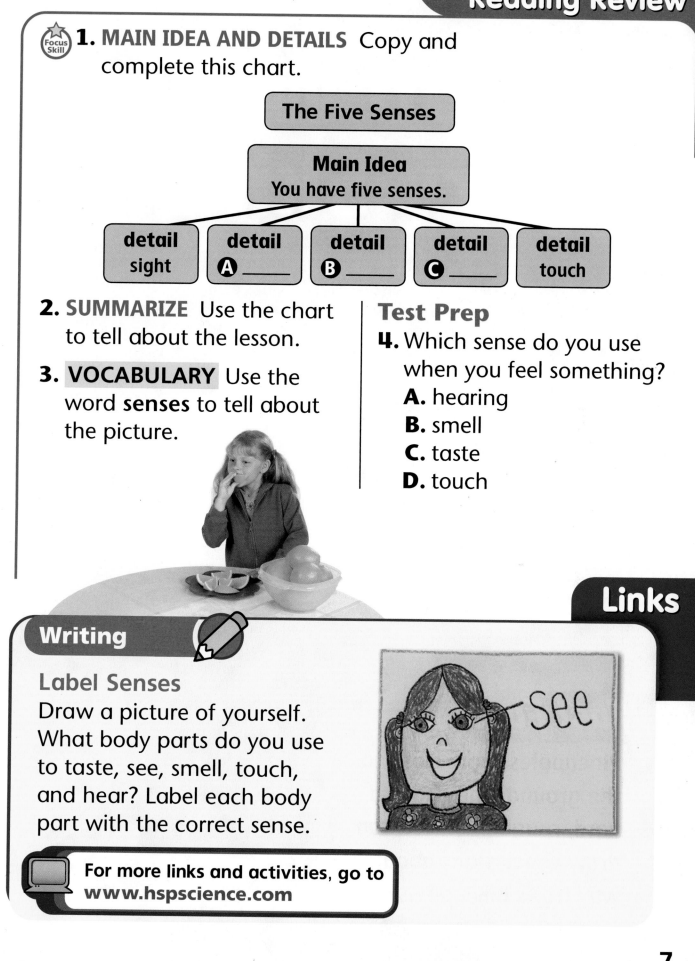

The Five Senses

Main Idea
You have five senses.

detail	detail	detail	detail	detail
sight	Ⓐ _____	Ⓑ _____	Ⓒ _____	touch

2. SUMMARIZE Use the chart to tell about the lesson.

3. VOCABULARY Use the word **senses** to tell about the picture.

Test Prep
4. Which sense do you use when you feel something?
  A. hearing
  B. smell
  C. taste
  D. touch

Links

Writing

Label Senses
Draw a picture of yourself. What body parts do you use to taste, see, smell, touch, and hear? Label each body part with the correct sense.

see

For more links and activities, go to **www.hspscience.com**

2

How Do We Use Inquiry Skills?

Fast Fact

Pineapples grow close to the ground. They have a hard, rough peel. You can draw conclusions about why fruits have peels.

Fruit Protection

You need

• **fruits**

• **hand lens**

Step 1

Observe some fruits with a hand lens. Look at their peels.

Step 2

Observe the cut fruits with the hand lens. What is inside the fruit?

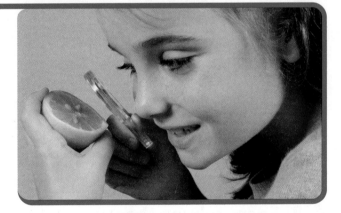

Step 3

Draw conclusions about why fruits have peels.

Inquiry Skill

To draw conclusions, you use information to figure out why something is the way it is.

Reading in Science

SI-1 Infer/Predict, SI-2 Explore student generated questions, SI-4 Work together/ communicate findings, SI-5 Draw conclusions, SI-8 Commmunicate work,

VOCABULARY

inquiry skills

★ **READING FOCUS SKILL**

MAIN IDEA AND DETAILS Look for details about the inquiry skills that scientists use.

Investigating

Everyone can do science! Scientists follow steps to test things they want to learn about.

1. Observe, and ask a question.

Ask questions. What do you want to know? You can work alone, with a partner, or in a small group.

Is a balloon filled with air heavier than a balloon without air in it?

2. Form a hypothesis.

Explore your questions. What do you think will happen?

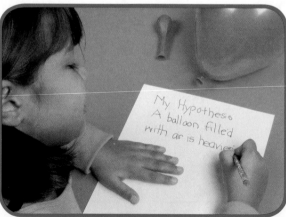

My Hypothesis
A balloon filled with air is heavier

SI-9 Describe and compare accurately, SK-1 Discover that experiments are repeatable, SK-2 Demonstrate good explanations, SK-3 Everyone can do science

3. Plan a fair test.

It is important to be fair. This will help you get correct answers to your questions.

I will tie these at the same spot on each end.

4. Do the test.

Try your test. Repeat it the same way. You should get the same answers.

5. Draw conclusions. Communicate what you learn.

Explain what you found out. Compare your answers with those of classmates. Share your answers by talking, drawing, or writing.

MAIN IDEA AND DETAILS What steps do scientists follow to test things?

Using Inquiry Skills

Scientists use inquiry skills when they do tests. **Inquiry skills** help people find out information.

communicate

classify

make a model

hypothesize

The red car will roll farther because it is heavier.

draw conclusions

13

compare

sequence

measure

egg

larva

pupa

butterfly comes out

adult butterfly

GO TEAM!

14

observe

predict

15

plan an investigation

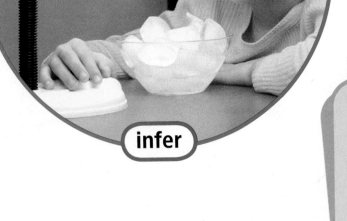
infer

How Far Will It Roll?

Get a ball. Predict how far it will go if you roll it across the floor. Mark that spot with tape. Roll the ball. Was your prediction right?

MAIN IDEA AND DETAILS

Focus Skill

What skills do scientists use when they do tests?

16

1. MAIN IDEA AND DETAILS Copy and complete this chart.

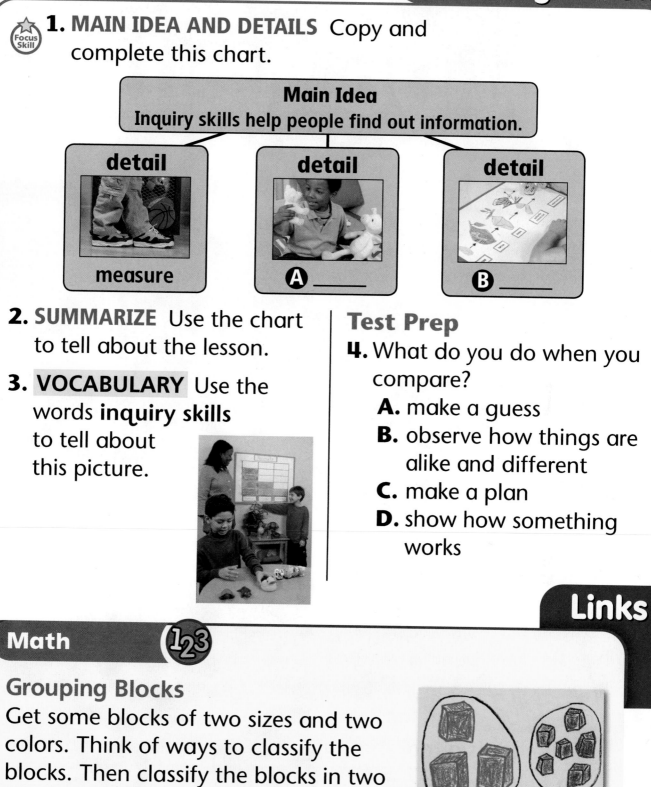

Main Idea
Inquiry skills help people find out information.

detail

measure

detail

Ⓐ _____

detail

Ⓑ _____

2. SUMMARIZE Use the chart to tell about the lesson.

3. VOCABULARY Use the words **inquiry skills** to tell about this picture.

Test Prep

4. What do you do when you compare?
  A. make a guess
  B. observe how things are alike and different
  C. make a plan
  D. show how something works

Links

Math

Grouping Blocks
Get some blocks of two sizes and two colors. Think of ways to classify the blocks. Then classify the blocks in two ways. Draw to show how you classified the blocks.

For more links and activities, go to
www.hspscience.com

How Do We Use Science Tools?

Compare Fruit

You need

- **strawberry**
- **pear**
- **balance**

Step 1

Put one piece of fruit on each side of a balance.

Step 2

Compare the masses of the fruits. Record what you see.

Step 3

Which fruit has less mass? Which has more mass?

Inquiry Skill

You **compare** when you observe ways things are alike and different.

VOCABULARY
science tools

Focus Skill **READING FOCUS SKILL**
MAIN IDEA AND DETAILS Look for details about science tools.

Using Science Tools

Scientists use tools to find out about things. You can use tools to find out about things, too. **Science tools** help people find information they need.

Some things have parts that are too small to see. You can use a hand lens or a magnifying box to help you see them.

hand lens and magnifying box

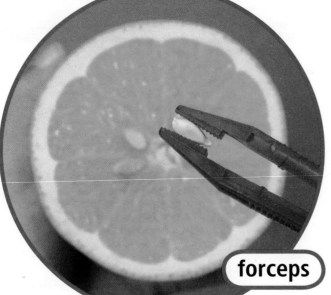

forceps

You can use forceps to help you separate things.

dropper

You can use a dropper to place drops of liquid.

You can use a measuring cup to measure liquid.

measuring cup

thermometer

You can use a thermometer to measure how hot or cold something is.

You can use a ruler to measure how long or tall an object is. You can use a measuring tape to measure around an object.

ruler and measuring tape

You can use a balance to measure the mass of an object.

balance

Insta-Lab

Measure It!
Use a tape measure to measure around your arm. Then measure around your leg. Compare the numbers. Which one is greater?

⭐ Focus Skill

MAIN IDEA AND DETAILS
How can you use science tools to find out information?

22

1. MAIN IDEA AND DETAILS Copy and complete this chart.

Science Tools

Main Idea
You can use science tools.

detail
You can use a **A** _____ and a magnifying box to help you see small objects.

detail
You can use a balance to measure the **B** _____ of an object.

detail
You can use a **C** _____ to measure how hot or cold something is.

2. DRAW CONCLUSIONS Draw conclusions about what you can use science tools to do.

3. VOCABULARY Use the words **science tools** to tell about the picture.

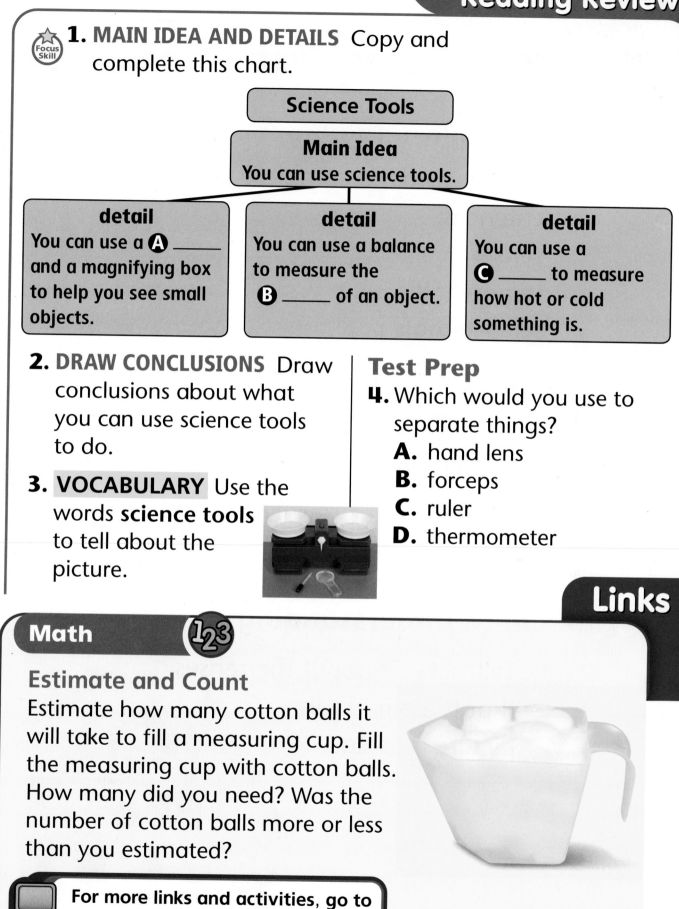

Test Prep

4. Which would you use to separate things?
   A. hand lens
   B. forceps
   C. ruler
   D. thermometer

Links

Math 123

Estimate and Count
Estimate how many cotton balls it will take to fill a measuring cup. Fill the measuring cup with cotton balls. How many did you need? Was the number of cotton balls more or less than you estimated?

For more links and activities, go to www.hspscience.com

23

Review and Test Preparation

Vocabulary Review

Use the words to complete the sentences.

senses p. 4

inquiry skills p. 12

science tools p. 20

1. You are using ___ when you compare and measure.

2. Smell is one of your five ___.

3. Scientists use ___ such as droppers and rulers.

Check Understanding

4. Tell **details** about the senses that the girl in this picture is using.

5. When you investigate something, what is the next step after you observe and ask questions?

A. Do the test.

B. Form a hypothesis.

C. Plan the test.

D. Draw conclusions and communicate what you learned.

Critical Thinking

6. Look at these science tools. Which would you use to make something look larger?

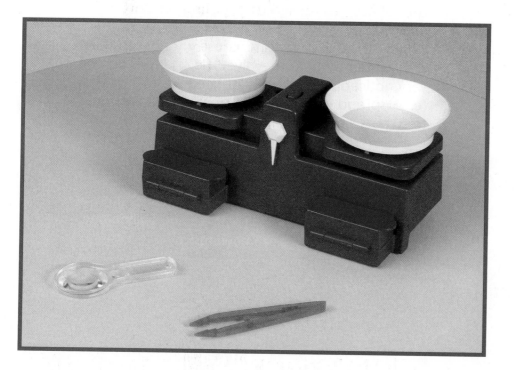

UNIT **A**

Columbus

Flint Ridge

Earth and Space Sciences

 The chapter and features in this unit address these Grade Level Indicators from the Ohio Academic Content Standards for Science.

Chapter **1**	**Natural Resources**
ES-1	Identify that resources are things that we get from the living (e.g., forests) and nonliving (e.g., minerals, water) environment and that resources are necessary to meet the needs and wants of a population.
ES-2	Explain that the supply of many resources is limited but the supply can be extended through careful use, decreased use, reusing and/or recycling.
ES-3	Explain that all organisms cause changes in the environment where they live; the changes can be very noticeable or slightly noticeable, fast or slow (e.g., spread of grass cover slowing soil erosion, tree roots slowly breaking sidewalks).

Unit A Ohio Expeditions

The investigations and experiences in this unit also address many of the Grade Level Indicators for standards in Science and Technology, Scientific Inquiry, and Scientific Ways of Knowing.

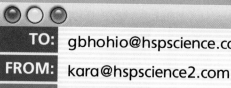
TO: gbhohio@hspscience.com
FROM: kara@hspscience2.com
RE: Flint Ridge

Dear Gabriel,

Today we saw Flint Ridge. It is a place where Native Americans got flint. They dug it out of the ground and used it to make tools.

See you,

Kara

Experiment!

Soil As you do this unit, you will find out about resources. Soil is one important resource. Plan and do a test. See what happens to soil when no plants grow in it.

1 Natural Resources

Vocabulary

natural resource

pollution

reduce

reuse

recycle

erosion

I wonder...

Where does water come from?

What do you wonder?

What Are Natural Resources?

Fast Fact

Long ago, people used moving air, or wind, to travel in sailing ships. You can observe ways people use natural resources.

All Around You

You need

- **crayons**

- **construction paper**

Step 1

Make a chart like this one.

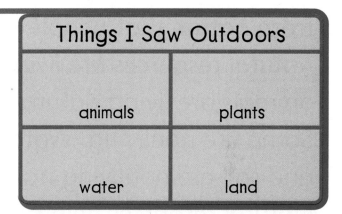

Things I Saw Outdoors	
animals	plants
water	land

Step 2

Go outside. **Observe** everything around you. Draw and label the things that belong in the chart.

Step 3

Share your chart with a classmate. Did you both **observe** the same things?

Inquiry Skill

When you **observe**, you use your senses to find out about things.

 ES-1 Identify and define resources, **SI-4** Work together/communicate findings, **SI-8** Communicate work, **SI-9** Describe and compare accurately

31

READING FOCUS SKILL

MAIN IDEA AND DETAILS Look for the main ideas about natural resources.

Natural Resources

A **natural resource** is anything from nature that people can use. Some natural resources are living. Plants and animals are living natural resources. Some are nonliving. Water, air, rocks, and soil are nonliving natural resources. Natural resources help people meet their needs and wants.

 MAIN IDEA AND DETAILS
What is a natural resource?

What natural resources do you see in this picture?

How are these people using water?

Water

Water is a natural resource that all living things need. People drink water and use it to clean and to cook. People travel on water, too.

⭐ **MAIN IDEA AND DETAILS**
What are some ways people use water?

Insta-Lab

Can Water Cool You?

Wrap one thermometer in a damp towel. Wrap another in a dry towel. Check them after 10 minutes. Which is cooler? How can you use water to keep your body cool?

Air

Air is a natural resource. You can not see air, but it is all around you. Many living things need air to live. People and many animals breathe air. People use air to fill things such as balloons. They also use air to make things move.

⭐ Focus Skill **MAIN IDEA AND DETAILS** What are some ways people use air?

How are these people using air?

Focus Skill

1. MAIN IDEA AND DETAILS Copy and complete this chart.

Main Idea
A **Ⓐ** _____ is anything from nature that people can use.

detail	**detail**	**detail**
People use **Ⓑ** _____ for drinking, cleaning, and cooking.	People and many animals breathe **Ⓒ** _____.	Plants, animals, rocks, and soil are some other natural resources.

2. DRAW CONCLUSIONS Is everything that people use a natural resource? Explain.

3. VOCABULARY Use the words **natural resource** to talk about this picture.

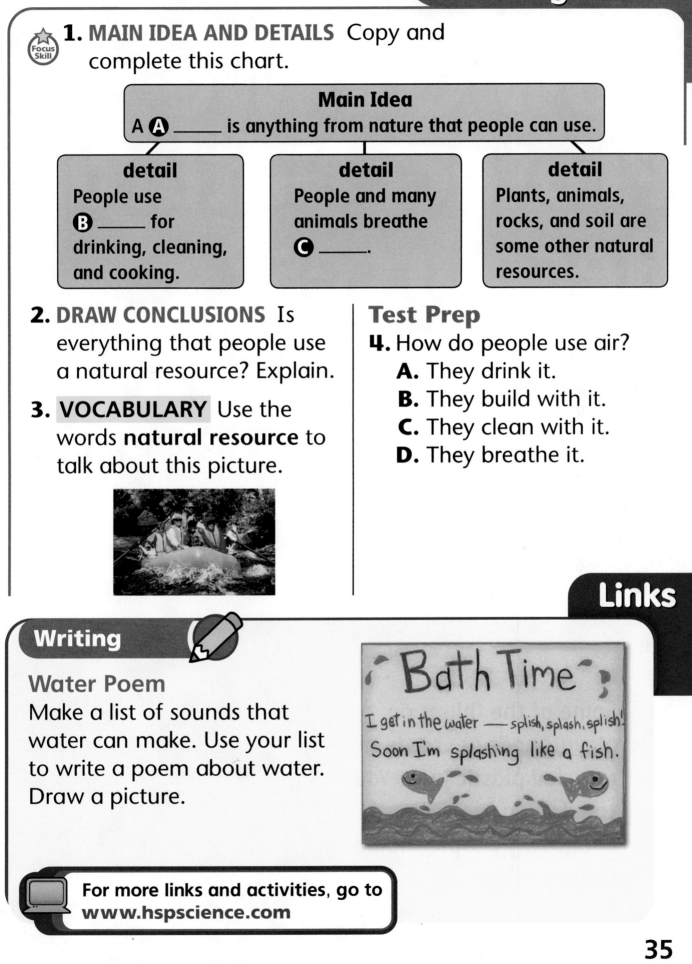

Test Prep

4. How do people use air?
  A. They drink it.
  B. They build with it.
  C. They clean with it.
  D. They breathe it.

Links

Writing

Water Poem
Make a list of sounds that water can make. Use your list to write a poem about water. Draw a picture.

Bath Time
I get in the water — splish, splash, splish!
Soon I'm splashing like a fish.

For more links and activities, go to www.hspscience.com

How Can We Protect Natural Resources?

Fast Fact

Some of the things on playgrounds are made from recycled plastic jugs! You can draw a conclusion about why people should recycle things.

What Happens to Trash?

You need

- lettuce
- napkin
- piece of foam cup
- pan of soil

Step 1

Bury the lettuce, the napkin, and the piece of foam cup in the soil.

Step 2

Water the soil every three days. After two weeks, dig up the things. What do you observe?

Step 3

Draw a conclusion. How could trash harm the land? Why?

Inquiry Skill

Use what you observe and what you know to **draw a conclusion.**

 ES-2 Explain resource conservation; **SI-5** Draw conclusions

VOCABULARY

pollution
reduce
reuse
recycle

 READING FOCUS SKILL

CAUSE AND EFFECT Look for ways people can take care of natural resources.

Taking Care of Resources

Pollution harms our natural resources. **Pollution** is waste that causes harm to land, water, and air. Pollution also causes harm to plants and animals.

People can pick up trash on land.

People can help take care of natural resources. They can put trash in its place. They can clean up trash. They can also walk or ride bikes instead of using cars. Cars and trucks make air pollution and use up natural resources.

Focus Skill **CAUSE AND EFFECT** What does pollution cause?

People can walk instead of using cars.

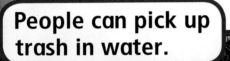

People can pick up trash in water.

Reduce, Reuse, Recycle

Some natural resources are limited. People can reduce, reuse, and recycle. This makes less trash. It also helps save natural resources.

To **reduce** something means to use less of it. People can use cloth bags. This reduces the number of paper and plastic bags that are used.

To **reuse** means to use something again. People can reuse food jars. The jars can hold pencils and other things.

To **recycle** means to use old things to make new things. People can recycle newpapers. The old papers can be made into new paper.

⭐ **CAUSE AND EFFECT** What effect does recycling have on the amount of trash?

Insta-Lab

Reuse an Egg Carton
Decorate an egg carton. Use it to store things you collect. You can keep different kinds of things in the different cups.

Ways to Save Resources

This family is saving resources.
How is each family member helping?

Turn off the lights when you leave a room.

Turn off the water when you do not need it.

Turn down the heat. Put on a sweater to stay warm.

Recycle.

For more links and activities, go to www.hspscience.com

Focus Skill

1. CAUSE AND EFFECT Copy and complete this chart.

Natural Resources

cause | **effect**

People make pollution. → Pollution harms our **A** _____.

People clean up **B** _____. → People take care of resources.

People **C** _____, reuse, and recycle. → People make less **D** _____.

2. DRAW CONCLUSIONS
How can you take care of resources at your home?

3. VOCABULARY Use the word **pollution** to talk about this picture.

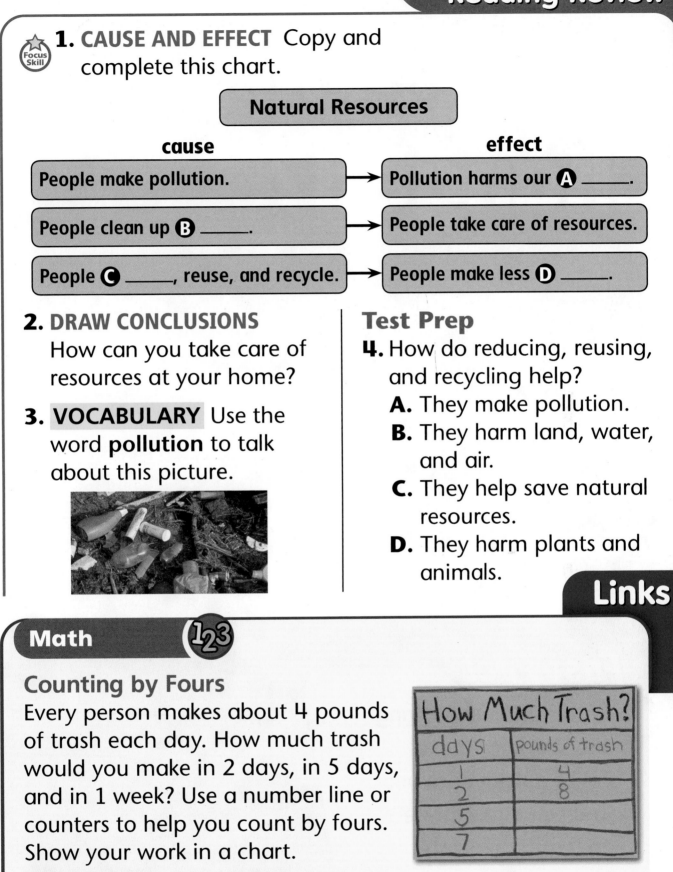

Test Prep

4. How do reducing, reusing, and recycling help?
  A. They make pollution.
  B. They harm land, water, and air.
  C. They help save natural resources.
  D. They harm plants and animals.

Links

Math 123

Counting by Fours
Every person makes about 4 pounds of trash each day. How much trash would you make in 2 days, in 5 days, and in 1 week? Use a number line or counters to help you count by fours. Show your work in a chart.

How Much Trash?	
days	pounds of trash
1	4
2	8
5	
7	

For more links and activities, go to **www.hspscience.com**

43

How Is Earth Changed?

Fast Fact

Water and wind change the shape of these rocks a little each year. You can make models to learn how water changes Earth.

Model Erosion

You need

• **damp soil**

• **tray**

• **water**

Step 1

Use soil to **make a model** of a mountain.

Step 2

Slowly pour water onto the top of the mountain.

Step 3

Observe. How does the mountain change? Tell how the **model** shows how water changes real mountains.

Inquiry Skill

Some changes take a long time. You can **make a model** to see how the changes happen.

ES-3 Explain how living things change Earth; **SI-8** Communicate work

45

VOCABULARY
erosion

 READING FOCUS SKILL

CAUSE AND EFFECT Look for some of the things that cause changes to Earth.

Changes to Earth

Living and nonliving things cause Earth to change. People build things. Some animals dig holes.

Wind and moving water also change Earth.

Focus Skill CAUSE AND EFFECT What are some things that cause Earth to change?

How are these living things changing Earth?

56

Fast Changes

Some changes are fast. You can see fast changes right away. Building a house is a fast change. Each day you can see that something is different.

 CAUSE AND EFFECT
What are some causes of fast changes?

Insta-Lab

Moving Water

Cut a cardboard tube in half the long way. Put the halves on a tray. Put something under one end of one half. Pour water into each half. Observe. Infer how the land's shape makes rivers flow fast or slowly.

Slow Changes

Some changes are slow. You can not always tell that something is different. Tree roots can break a sidewalk. This change takes a long time.

Moving water also slowly changes the land. It carries rocks and soil to new places. This is called **erosion**.

Focus Skill **CAUSE AND EFFECT** What is the effect of planting grass?

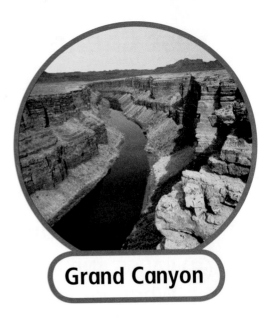

Grand Canyon

Some people plant grass to slow erosion.

tree roots breaking sidewalk

Focus Skill

1. CAUSE AND EFFECT Copy and complete this chart.

cause   **effect**

| People build things. | → | **A** _____ changes. |

| Some changes are **B** _____. | → | You see these changes right away. |

| Some changes are **C** _____. | → | You can not always tell that something is different. |

2. SUMMARIZE Use the chart to summarize this lesson.

3. VOCABULARY Use the word **erosion** to tell about this picture.

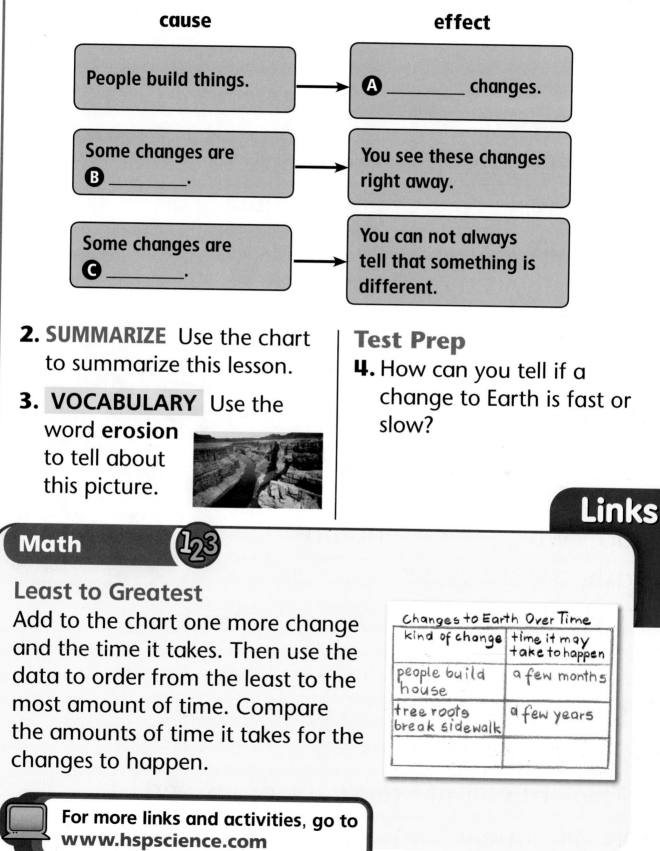

Test Prep

4. How can you tell if a change to Earth is fast or slow?

Links

Math 1 2 3

Least to Greatest

Add to the chart one more change and the time it takes. Then use the data to order from the least to the most amount of time. Compare the amounts of time it takes for the changes to happen.

Changes to Earth Over Time	
kind of change	time it may take to happen
people build house	a few months
tree roots break sidewalk	a few years

For more links and activities, go to www.hspscience.com

49

Be Earth's Friend

Earth Day is a time for people to think about taking care of Earth. People can keep plants and animals healthy. They can also help keep Earth clean.

1. Reduce.

Each person in the United States makes about 2 kilograms (4 pounds) of trash every day! So landfills, or places where people dump trash, are starting to get full.

Look for ways to reduce your trash.

2. Reuse.

Some trash in landfills could be used for other things.

Think of ways to reuse things instead of throwing them away.

50

3. Recycle.

Paper takes up the most space in landfills. It can be recycled to make new paper.

Put your old newspapers in your recycling bin, or take them to a recycling center.

4. Respect.

People need to respect, or care for, Earth. One way to show respect for Earth is to use fewer resources.

Respect Earth by turning off the water while you brush your teeth.

THINK ABOUT IT

What does Earth Day teach people about taking care of Earth?

Find out more! Log on to
www.hspscience.com

ES-1 Identify and define resources; **ES-2** Explain resource conservation

Studying Rivers

Dr. Ruth Patrick is a nature scientist. Her father taught her to love plants, streams, and rivers.

Dr. Patrick studies the plants and animals that live in rivers. She knows that pollution can harm a river. She has made a list of things scientists can check to see if a river is polluted. Dr. Patrick helps keep our rivers clean.

You Can Do It!

Making Water Clean

What to Do

1. Mix salt and water in one cup. Taste the salt water. Pour it into the tub.

2. Put the other cup in the tub. Cover the tub with plastic, using the rubber band. Put marbles on top.

3. Put the tub in the sun for two hours. Then taste the water that is in the cup.

Materials

- salt
- 2 cups
- water
- spoon
- tub of sand
- plastic wrap
- rubber band
- marbles

Draw Conclusions

What do you think happened to the water?

Too Much Packaging

Some foods come in packages that make lots of trash. Look at foods in your kitchen. Draw those that have too much packaging. Then draw to show how these foods could have less packaging.

Juice boxes have too much packaging. You could buy jars of juice.

Review and Test Preparation

Vocabulary Review

Use each word or words to tell about the picture.

1.  **natural resource** p. 32

2.  **pollution** p. 38

3.  **recycle** p. 41

4.  **erosion** p. 48

Check Understanding

5. Tell details about the natural [Focus Skill] resources in this picture.

6. What is one thing people may do to slow down soil erosion?

   A. build things

   B. dig holes

   C. carry rock and soil to new places

   D. plant grass

7. What harms natural resources?

   F. air   **H.** pollution

   G. water   **J.** recycling

Critical Thinking

8. You want to take care of resources in your school. Write a plan. Tell each thing you would do. Tell why each thing would help.

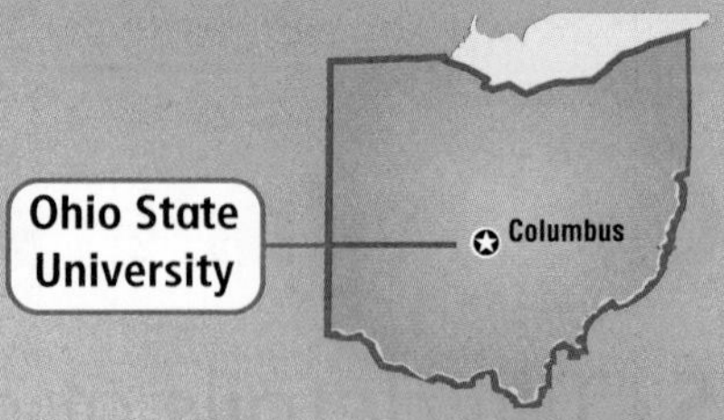

Ohio State University → Columbus

UNIT A OHIO EXPEDITIONS

Orton Hall

Orton Hall is a special building. Can you see what it is made of? It was built with 40 kinds of rocks! All the rocks came from Ohio.

Rock can be carved. What shapes do you see here?

Orton Hall

People use rocks for many things. Builders used large rocks to make the walls of Orton Hall. They used cement to hold the large rocks together. Cement is made of crushed rock.

Can you see many kinds of rocks?

Think and Do

1. SCIENCE AND TECHNOLOGY Think about the story of the three little pigs. What did the pigs use to build their houses? Which house was the strongest? Do you think Orton Hall is a strong building? Do an experiment with straw, a stick of wood, and a brick. Work with a partner to find out which is the strongest.

2. SCIENTIFIC THINKING What is your school building made of? Why do you think these things were chosen to make your school?

Belmont County

Columbus

Belmont County Coal Mine

There is a lot of coal in Ohio. Coal is like a rock. It is black and hard. Coal is found under the ground. It is an important resource. Belmont County has the most coal in Ohio.

an energy station

coal

Coal is used to produce electricity. First, miners take the coal out of the ground. Next, the coal is shipped to an energy station. Then, the coal is burned. It is very hot. Last, the heat from the coal helps produce electricity.

Coal looks like this before it is mined.

Think and Do

I. **SCIENCE AND TECHNOLOGY** Why do we need electricity? How do we use it? Walk through your school. Make a list of the things that use electricity.

2. **SCIENTIFIC THINKING** Someday all our coal may be used up. How can we make our coal last longer? Make a poster to show ways we can save electricity.

ES-1 Identify and define resources; **ST-4** Explore energy use; **ST-5** Explore energy conservation; **ST-7** Explore stages in building

59

Cleveland

Columbus

The First Oil Well

In 1814, two men were digging for salt. They found salt. They also found oil. They put a hollow log in the ground. It went down to where the oil was. Then they pumped out the oil. This was the first oil well.

This is what an oil well looks like today.

Like coal, oil is used for energy. We use oil's energy to make things go. Oil is made into gasoline. We put gas into cars, trucks, buses, and airplanes. The gasoline makes their engines work.

Most lawnmowers use gasoline.

How many of these things use gasoline?

Think and Do

I. **SCIENCE AND TECHNOLOGY** Draw a picture to show ways people can travel without using gas.

2. **SCIENTIFIC THINKING** Make a chart that shows how coal and oil are alike and different.

 ES-1 Identify and define resources; **ES-2** Explain resource conservation; **ST-4** Explore energy use; **ST-5** Explore energy conservation

61

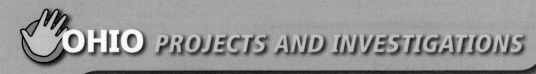

Are All Rocks the Same?

UNIT A OHIO EXPEDITIONS

Materials
- rocks
- hand lens
- balance
- measuring tape

What to Do
1. Look at all the rocks.
2. Sort the rocks into groups.
3. Sort them in new ways.

Draw Conclusions
1. How are the rocks alike and different?
2. What could you use a rock to make?

Trash Tally

Materials
- large box

What to Do

1. Place a large box next to your class trash can.

2. Put paper, plastic, and aluminum trash in the box. Put food and other messy trash in the trash can.

3. At the end of one day, look in the box.

4. At the end of one week, look in the box.

Draw Conclusions

1. What class trash could you reuse? Make a list.

2. What class trash could you recycle? Make a list.

 PS-1 Classify objects by properties; **ST-3** Identify recyclables; **SK-2** Demonstrate good explanations; **SK-3** Everyone can do science

63

UNIT **B**

Franklin Park Conservatory

Columbus

Life Sciences

The chapters and features in this unit address these Grade Level Indicators from the Ohio Academic Content Standards for Science.

Unit B Ohio Expeditions

The investigations and experiences in this unit also address many of the Grade Level Indicators for standards in Science and Technology, Scientific Inquiry, and Scientific Ways of Knowing.

TO: hmuohio@hspscience.com
FROM: lashonda@hspscience2.com
RE: Franklin Park Conservatory

Hi Hunter,

Franklin Park Conservatory is a big building with many rooms. Each room has different plants. One has desert plants. I forgot I was inside a building!

Lashonda

Experiment!

Habitats As you do this unit, you will see where some plants and animals live. Plan and do a test. Find out how animal coverings help them live where they do.

Chapter 2

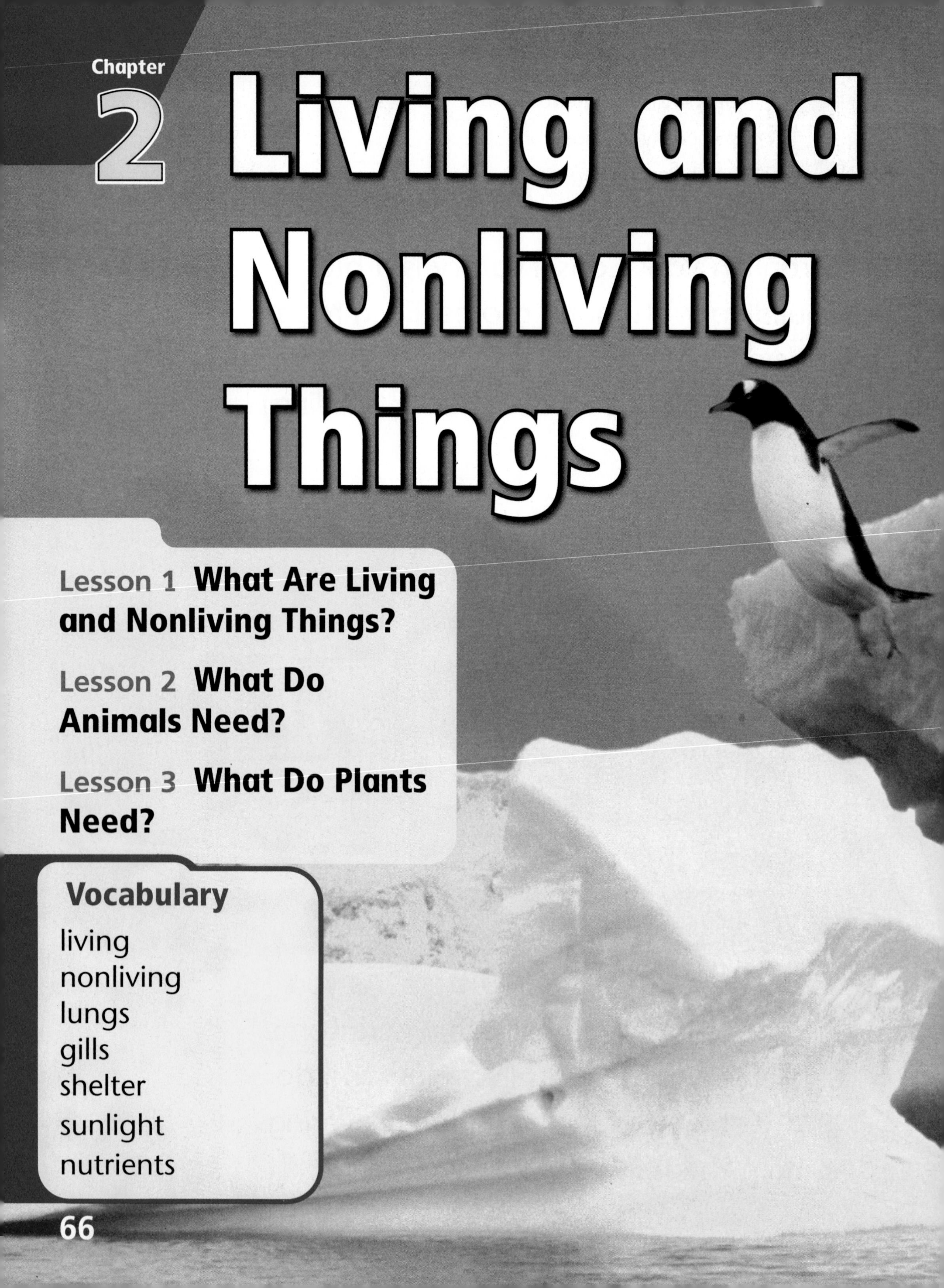

Living and Nonliving Things

Lesson 1 **What Are Living and Nonliving Things?**

Lesson 2 **What Do Animals Need?**

Lesson 3 **What Do Plants Need?**

Vocabulary

living
nonliving
lungs
gills
shelter
sunlight
nutrients

I wonder...

How do penguins stay warm?

What do **you** wonder?

What Are Living and Nonliving Things?

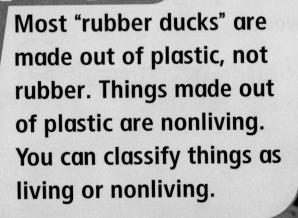

Fast Fact

Most "rubber ducks" are made out of plastic, not rubber. Things made out of plastic are nonliving. You can classify things as living or nonliving.

Living and Nonliving Things

You need

- **mealworm**
- **rock**
- **bran meal and box**
- **hand lens**

Step 1

Put the mealworm, rock, and bran meal in a box. Observe with the hand lens.

Step 2

Does the mealworm eat or move? Does the rock eat or move? Draw what you see.

Step 3

Classify the mealworm and the rock as living things or nonliving things.

Inquiry Skill

When you **classify** things, you can see how they are alike and different.

VOCABULARY	(Focus Skill) **READING FOCUS SKILL**
living nonliving	**COMPARE AND CONTRAST** Look for ways living things and nonliving things are alike and different.

Living and Nonliving Things

Living things need food, water, and air. They all grow and change. Plants, animals, and people are living things.

> Which things in this picture are living? Which are nonliving?

wolf

rocks

Nonliving things do not need food, water, or air. They do not grow. Rocks and water are nonliving things.

Focus Skill **COMPARE AND CONTRAST** How are all nonliving things alike?

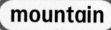

mountain

plants

Insta-Lab

Compare Living Things
Draw a living thing. Then compare your picture with a partner's picture. Are both things living? Talk about how you know.

water

Classify Living and Nonliving Things

You can classify things as living or nonliving. Living things need food, water, and air. They grow and change. If something is not like living things in these two ways, then it is nonliving.

Living	Nonliving

 COMPARE AND CONTRAST Look at the chart. How are the living things different from the nonliving things?

72

Focus Skill

1. COMPARE AND CONTRAST Copy and complete this chart.

Living Things	Nonliving Things
They need **A** _____.	They do not need food.
They need water.	They do not need **B** _____.
They need **C** _____.	They do not need **D** _____.
They grow and **E** _____.	They do not **F** _____.

2. SUMMARIZE Use the chart to write a lesson summary.

3. VOCABULARY Use the words **living** and **nonliving** to talk about the picture.

Test Prep

4. Tell how these nonliving things are alike.

ball   cup

rock   water

Links

Writing

Writing About Animals
Draw a toy animal and a real animal. Label them. Then compare the animals. Write about how they are alike and how they are different.

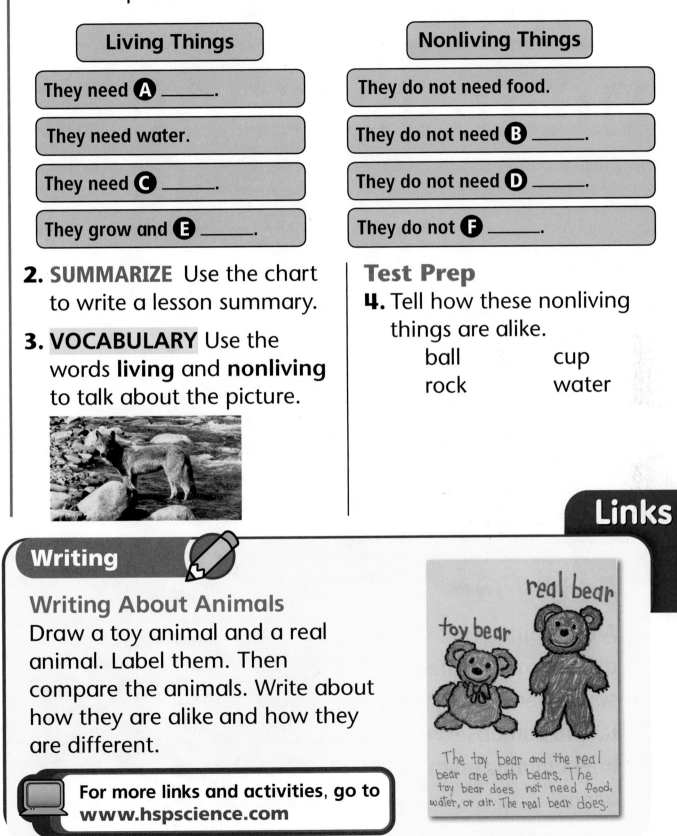

real bear

toy bear

The toy bear and the real bear are both bears. The toy bear does not need food, water, or air. The real bear does.

For more links and activities, go to www.hspscience.com

73

What Do Animals Need?

Fast Fact

A caterpillar eats almost all the time. It sheds its skin when it outgrows it. You can observe how animals meet their needs.

Observe an Animal Home

You need

- plastic box and gloves
- soil, twig, leaf, rocks
- water in a bottle cap
- small animals

Step 1

Put the soil, twig, leaf, rocks, and water in the box. Add the animals.

Step 2

Observe. Draw what you see.

Step 3

Explain how the home you made gives the animals food, water, and a place to live.

Inquiry Skill

Observe the animals in their home to see how they meet their needs.

VOCABULARY

lungs
gills
shelter

(Focus Skill) READING FOCUS SKILL

MAIN IDEA AND DETAILS Look for the four things all animals need to live.

Animals Need Food and Water

Animals need food to live and grow. Pandas eat bamboo.

Animals need water, too. Zebras and giraffes drink from ponds. They also get water from foods they eat.

(Focus Skill) MAIN IDEA AND DETAILS What are two things animals need to live?

panda

giraffe

zebra

76

Animals Need Air

All animals need air. They have body parts that help them breathe. Giraffes and zebras have lungs. **Lungs** help people and some animals breathe air. Fish have gills. **Gills** take air from water.

⭐ **MAIN IDEA AND DETAILS**
Focus Skill
What are two body parts animals use to get air?

Insta-Lab

Pet Food Survey
Take a survey. List some pet foods. Then ask classmates what their pets eat. Put a tally mark next to each food. Which food is eaten by most children's pets?

Animals Need Shelter

Most animals need shelter. A **shelter** is a place where an animal can be safe. Some birds use a tree as shelter. A hole in the ground is a shelter for foxes.

 MAIN IDEA AND DETAILS
Why does a bird use a tree as shelter?

owl

foxes

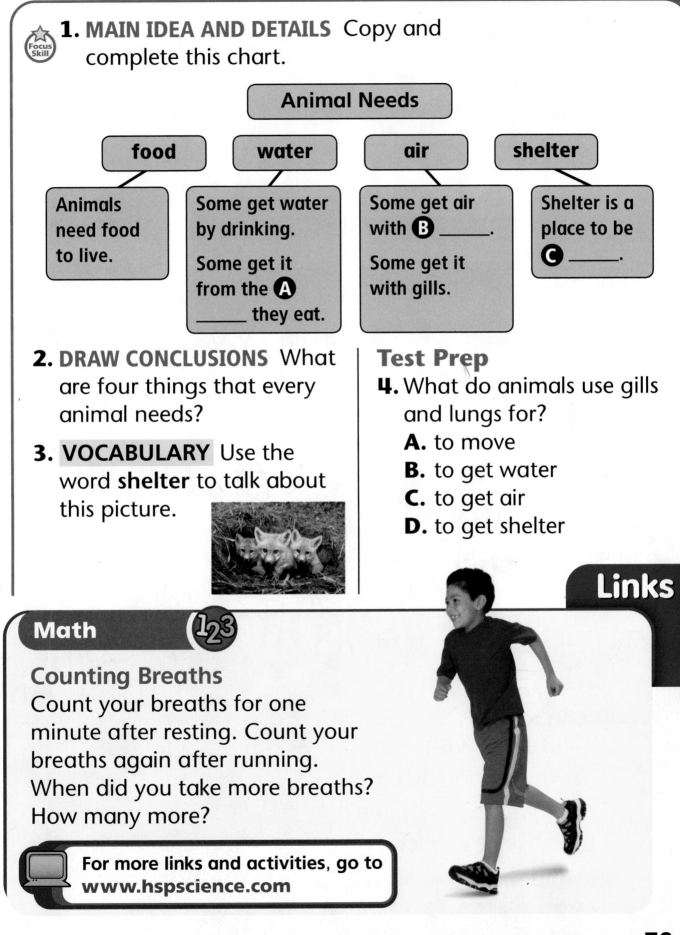

1. **MAIN IDEA AND DETAILS** Copy and complete this chart.

Animal Needs

food

Animals need food to live.

water

Some get water by drinking.

Some get it from the **A** _____ they eat.

air

Some get air with **B** _____.

Some get it with gills.

shelter

Shelter is a place to be **C** _____.

2. **DRAW CONCLUSIONS** What are four things that every animal needs?

3. **VOCABULARY** Use the word **shelter** to talk about this picture.

Test Prep

4. What do animals use gills and lungs for?

   A. to move

   B. to get water

   C. to get air

   D. to get shelter

Links

Math

Counting Breaths
Count your breaths for one minute after resting. Count your breaths again after running. When did you take more breaths? How many more?

For more links and activities, go to www.hspscience.com

What Do Plants Need?

Fast Fact

Orchids have roots that take water from the air. Predict what will happen if there is not enough water in the air.

What Plants Need

You need

- index cards
- 2 small plants
- spray bottle

Step 1

Label the plants. Put both plants in a sunny place.

Step 2

Water only one plant each day. **Predict** what will happen to each plant.

Step 3

After four days, check the plants. Did you **predict** correctly?

Inquiry Skill

To **predict**, use what you know to make a good guess about what will happen.

VOCABULARY
sunlight
nutrients

(Focus Skill) **READING FOCUS SKILL**

CAUSE AND EFFECT Look for all the things that cause plants to grow.

Light, Air, and Water

A plant needs light, air, and water to make its own food. The food helps the plant grow and stay healthy. A plant also needs water to move the food to all its parts.

sunlight

air

water

Plants take in **sunlight**, or light from the sun. They take in water mostly from the soil.

 CAUSE AND EFFECT
Focus Skill
What would happen to a plant that did not have light, air, or water?

Make a Model Plant
Use paper, clay, craft sticks, and other art materials to make a model plant. Then tell about what a real plant needs to live.

Soil

Plants take in nutrients from the soil. **Nutrients** are minerals that plants use to make their food.

 CAUSE AND EFFECT Why does a plant need nutrients?

soil

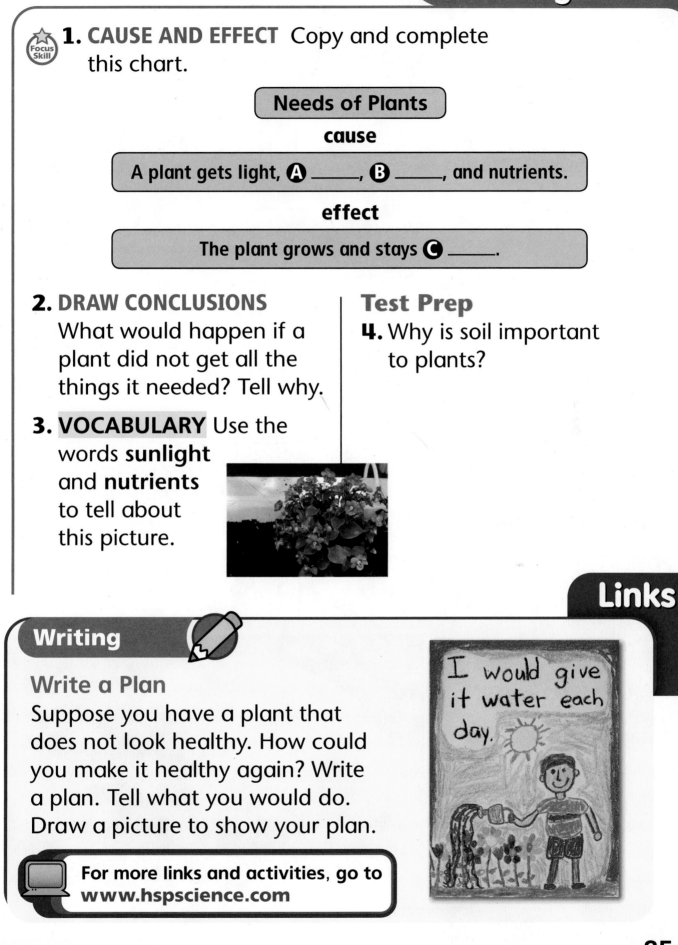

1. CAUSE AND EFFECT Copy and complete this chart.

Needs of Plants

cause

A plant gets light, **A** _____, **B** _____, and nutrients.

effect

The plant grows and stays **C** _____.

2. DRAW CONCLUSIONS What would happen if a plant did not get all the things it needed? Tell why.

3. VOCABULARY Use the words **sunlight** and **nutrients** to tell about this picture.

Test Prep

4. Why is soil important to plants?

Links

Writing

Write a Plan

Suppose you have a plant that does not look healthy. How could you make it healthy again? Write a plan. Tell what you would do. Draw a picture to show your plan.

For more links and activities, go to www.hspscience.com

I would give it water each day.

85

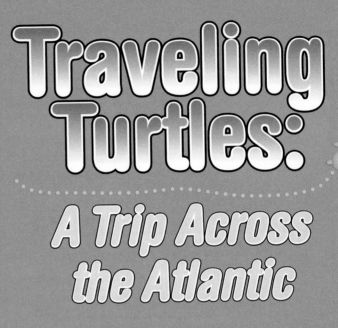

Traveling Turtles:
A Trip Across the Atlantic

In late spring, huge sea turtles crawl onto a beach in Florida. Each turtle digs a nest in the sand. The mother turtle then lays about 100 eggs. Two months later, tiny turtles hatch.

The young turtles crawl out of their holes and into the ocean.

A Long Trip

The tiny turtles set out on a long trip. They swim across the Atlantic Ocean and back again. The trip takes between five and ten years. The trip is thousands of miles long.

Scientists wanted to know how the turtles made their way across the ocean. To find out, scientists put "bathing suits" on some young sea turtles. The suits were tied to special machines. The machines can follow how the turtles swim.

THINK ABOUT IT

How long will it take for a young turtle to swim across the Atlantic Ocean?

Find out more! Log on to
www.hspscience.com

Feeding Time

Chloe Ruiz went to the petting zoo with her family. Chloe saw pigs, horses, and cows.

The people at the zoo asked Chloe if she wanted to help feed a young cow. A young cow is called a calf.

Chloe fed the calf milk. She used a bottle to feed the calf. She knows the calf needs to drink lots of milk to help it grow.

Which Foods Birds Eat

What to Do

1. Put bread crumbs in one pie plate. Put fruit in the other.
2. Put both plates on a table outside.
3. Observe the birds that eat from each plate. Draw pictures to record your observations.

Materials
- 2 foil pie plates
- bread crumbs
- chopped apples and grapes

Draw Conclusions
Do different birds eat different foods? How do you know?

Animals and Their Young

Mammals and most birds care for their young. Choose one. Find out how it helps its young. Make models to show how the animal cares for its young.

LS-1 Explore organisms' basic needs

Review and Test Preparation

Vocabulary Review

Match each word to its picture.
Tell how you know.

A.

1. gills p. 77

B.

2. shelter p. 78

C.

3. sunlight p. 83

4. nutrients p. 84

D.

Check Understanding

5. Compare. How are plants and animals alike?

   A. They are nonliving things.

   B. They need water and air.

   C. They need shelter.

   D. They need soil.

6. What happens to a plant that gets air, light, water, and nutrients? Tell how you know.

Critical Thinking

7. Compare the pigs. Which one is living? Which is not? Tell how you know.

8. Think about getting a pet you want. Draw a picture of the pet. List each thing it needs. Tell how you would help it meet its needs.

Chapter 3

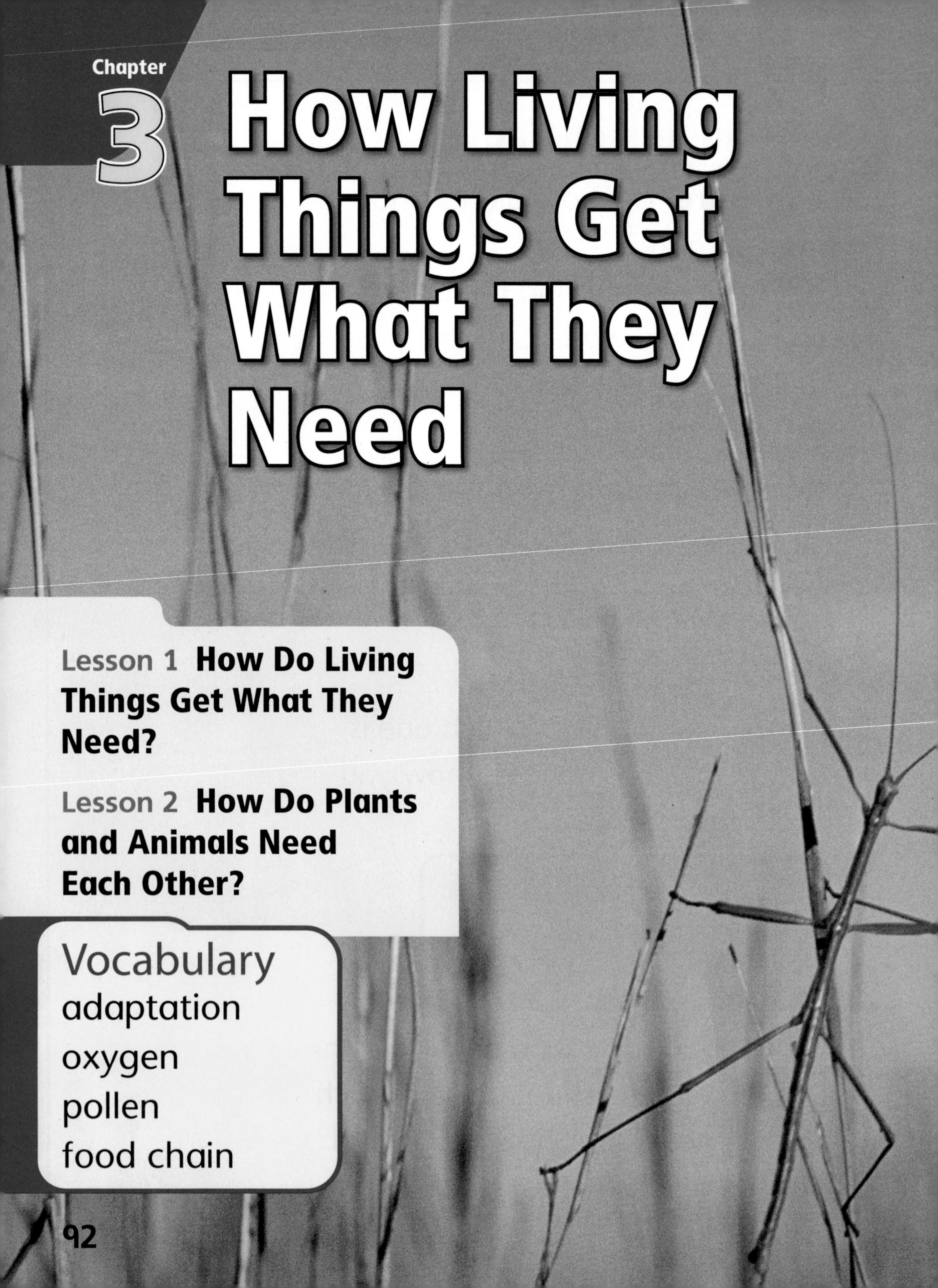

How Living Things Get What They Need

Lesson 1 How Do Living Things Get What They Need?

Lesson 2 How Do Plants and Animals Need Each Other?

Vocabulary

adaptation

oxygen

pollen

food chain

I wonder...

Why do these insects look like plants?

What do you wonder?

How Do Living Things Get What They Need?

Fast Fact

An alligator has eyes on the top of its head. Draw a conclusion about how this might help an alligator.

Some Animals Hide

You need

- **colored paper clips**
- **colored paper**

Step 1

Put the clips on a sheet of colored paper. Which clips are hard to see?

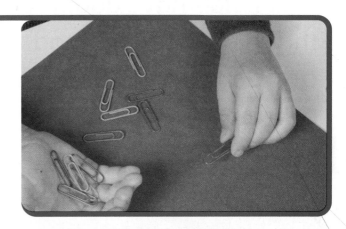

Step 2

Put the clips on a sheet of paper of a different color. Which clips are hard to see now?

Step 3

Draw a conclusion about how color helps some animals hide.

Inquiry Skill

To **draw conclusions,** think about why some of the clips were hard to see.

LS-3 Explore body parts to get food; SI-5 Draw conclusions

95

LS-2 Explain where food comes from; **LS-3** Explore body parts to get food

VOCABULARY
adaptation

 READING FOCUS SKILL

MAIN IDEA AND DETAILS Look for how living things get food and the details that tell more about it.

How Animals Get Food

Animals have adaptations that help them get food. An **adaptation** is a body part or behavior that helps a living thing.

Adaptations may help animals catch food. An eagle can see food from high in the air. A shark can smell it from far away. A cheetah runs fast to catch it.

eagle

sharp teeth

cheetah

Camouflage

Some animals have an adaptation called camouflage. Camouflage is an animal's color or pattern that helps it hide. It helps an animal stay safe or find food.

For more links and activities, go to **www.hspscience.com**

Some adaptations help animals eat. Sharp teeth help lions tear meat. Flat teeth help horses chew grass.

MAIN IDEA AND DETAILS
How do adaptations help animals get food?

flat teeth

Insta-Lab

Observe Beaks

Put crumbs from lunch on a tray. Put the tray outside where you can see it. Then watch for birds. What birds do you see? How does each one use its beak to eat?

How People Get Food

People get food from plants and animals. They make bread with wheat grown on farms. They get eggs from chickens. They fish for seafood.

Adaptations help people eat, too. People have sharp teeth and flat teeth. Sharp teeth tear meat. Flat teeth chew other foods.

Focus Skill **MAIN IDEA AND DETAILS** How do teeth help people eat?

What are some ways people get food?

98

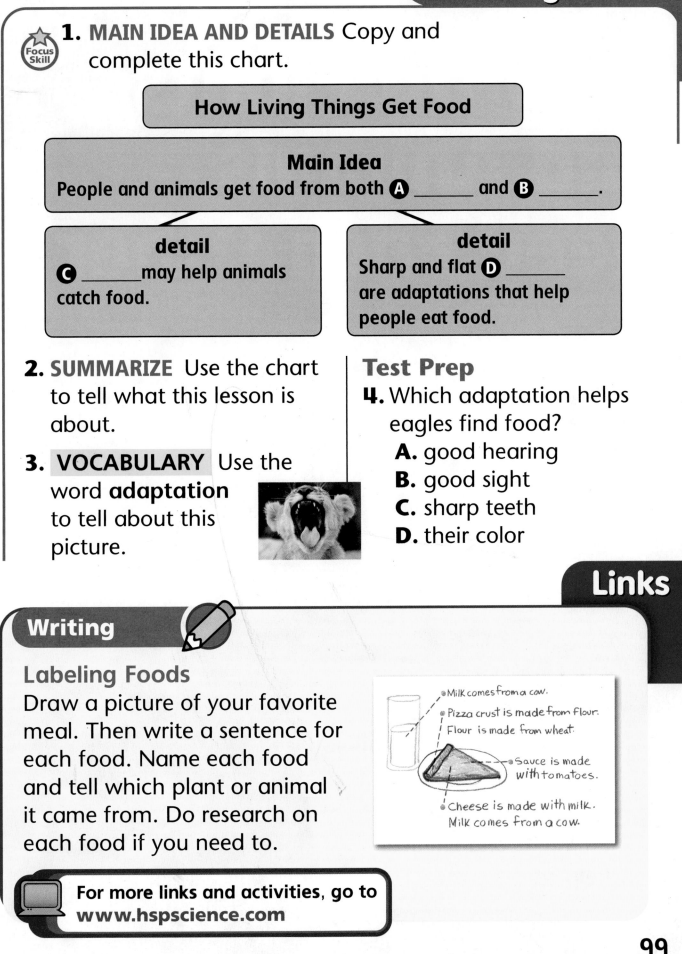

Focus Skill

1. MAIN IDEA AND DETAILS Copy and complete this chart.

How Living Things Get Food

Main Idea
People and animals get food from both **A** _____ and **B** _____.

detail
C _____ may help animals catch food.

detail
Sharp and flat **D** _____ are adaptations that help people eat food.

2. SUMMARIZE Use the chart to tell what this lesson is about.

3. VOCABULARY Use the word **adaptation** to tell about this picture.

Test Prep

4. Which adaptation helps eagles find food?
   A. good hearing
   B. good sight
   C. sharp teeth
   D. their color

Links

Writing

Labeling Foods
Draw a picture of your favorite meal. Then write a sentence for each food. Name each food and tell which plant or animal it came from. Do research on each food if you need to.

• Milk comes from a cow.
• Pizza crust is made from flour. Flour is made from wheat.
• Sauce is made with tomatoes.
• Cheese is made with milk. Milk comes from a cow.

For more links and activities, go to www.hspscience.com

How Do Plants and Animals Need Each Other?

Fast Fact

Flowers make food that bees eat. Bees carry pollen, which helps plants make seeds. What other ways do plants and animals help each other?

Animals in a Tree

You need

● **hand lens**

Step 1

Find a tree with your class. **Observe** it with a hand lens. Record what you see.

Step 2

Sit quietly and **observe**. Record what animals in your tree are doing.

Step 3

How did animals use the tree? Explain what you **observed**.

Inquiry Skill

Use your senses to help you **observe**.

 LS-4 Investigate animal/plant interactions, **SI-6** Use tools and equipment, **SK-2** Demonstrate good explanations

Reading in Science

VOCABULARY

oxygen
pollen
food chain

READING FOCUS SKILL

MAIN IDEA AND DETAILS Look for the main ideas about how animals use plants and help plants.

Animals Use Plants

Animals use plants to meet their needs. Some live in plants or use them to make homes. Plants are good places for animals to hide in, too.

deer hiding behind trees

heron hiding in grass

beaver building a dam

Some animals help plants by carrying seeds. They take seeds to new places. The seeds may grow into new plants there.

⭐ **MAIN IDEA AND DETAILS**

How can animals help plants make new plants?

squirrel carrying seeds

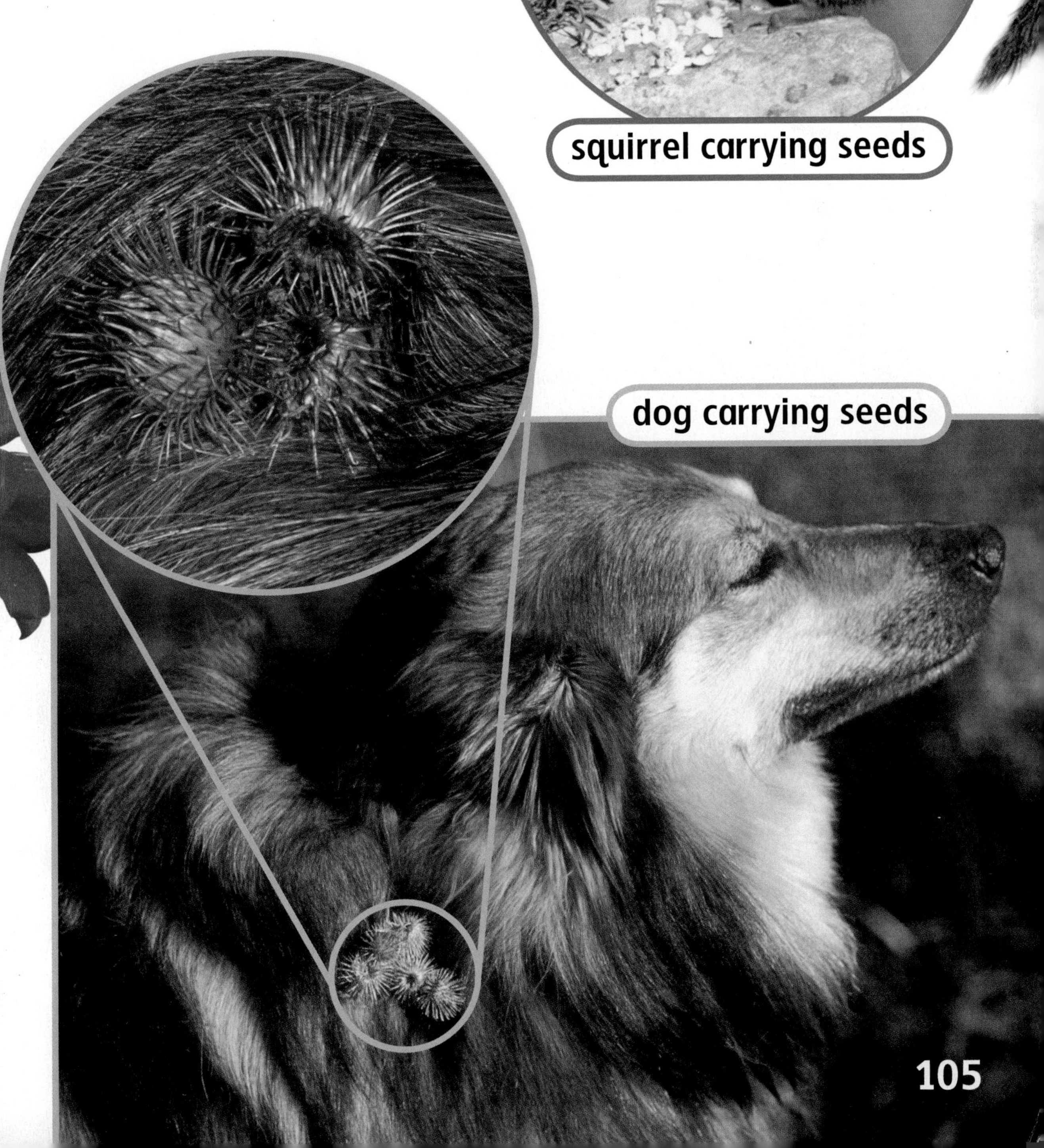

dog carrying seeds

Food Chain

Animals can be grouped by what they eat. Some animals eat plants. Some eat other animals. A **food chain** shows how animals and plants are linked.

★ **MAIN IDEA AND DETAILS**
What does a food chain show?

Last, a bear eats the trout.

Next, a rainbow trout eats the stonefly.

First, a stonefly eats part of a plant.

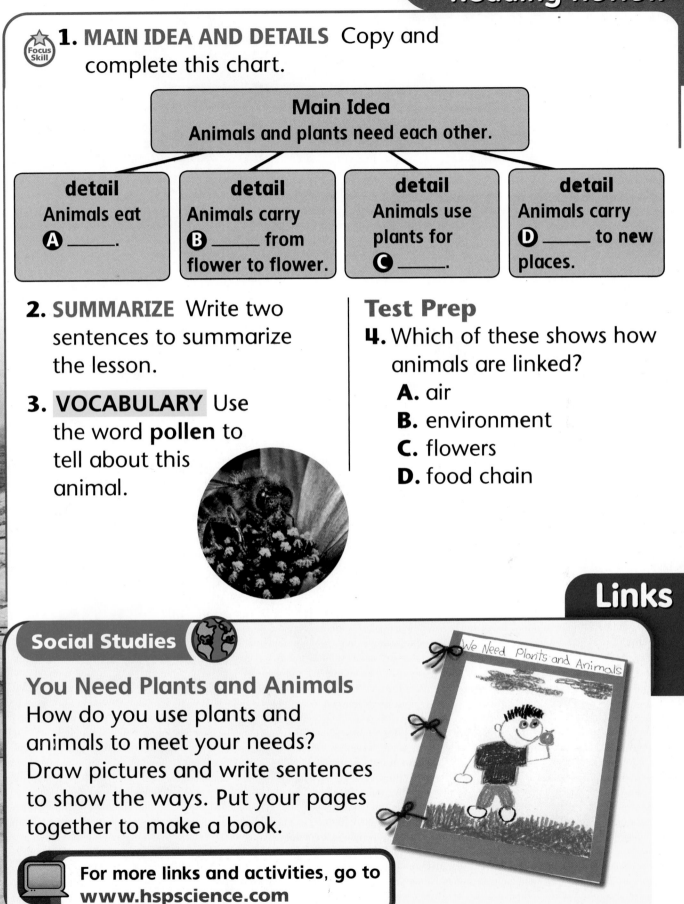

Focus Skill

1. MAIN IDEA AND DETAILS Copy and complete this chart.

Main Idea
Animals and plants need each other.

detail	**detail**	**detail**	**detail**
Animals eat **A** _____.	Animals carry **B** _____ from flower to flower.	Animals use plants for **C** _____.	Animals carry **D** _____ to new places.

2. SUMMARIZE Write two sentences to summarize the lesson.

3. VOCABULARY Use the word **pollen** to tell about this animal.

Test Prep

4. Which of these shows how animals are linked?
   A. air
   B. environment
   C. flowers
   D. food chain

Links

Social Studies

You Need Plants and Animals

How do you use plants and animals to meet your needs? Draw pictures and write sentences to show the ways. Put your pages together to make a book.

We Need Plants and Animals

For more links and activities, go to www.hspscience.com

SCIENCE Spin™ from WEEKLY READER®
Technology

Now You See It, Now You Don't

Do you ever wish you
...way an

...e ani...als
...food...

...teacher. He lives in
Japan. Tachi made
a coat to show how
things can be hidden.

The coat is covered
by many tiny glass
beads. The beads
reflect light. This
makes it seem as if
you can see through
a person wearing
the coat.

THINK ABOUT IT
How is this coat like
an animal's
camouflage?

Seeing into the Future

Susumi Tachi's idea might
be used in many ways.
Doctors could use tools with
the beads on them. Then
they could see through the
tools when they operate.

Find out more! Log on to
www.hspscience.com

LS-5 Recognize influence of seasons

Where Are All the Butterflies?

People often see monarch butterflies in fall. These insects leave places in the north when the weather turns cold. They fly to warmer places in the south. Scientists want to know why.

Emma Griffiths helped scientists count butterflies. Emma helped by scooping up butterflies in a net. Then scientists put a tiny tag on each insect. The tag will show other scientists that these butterflies came from Connecticut.

What Makes Seeds Stick?

Materials
- foam ball
- glue
- rough materials

What to Do

1. Find some seeds. Which ones do you think might stick to animals?

2. Make a model of a seed that will stick to things.

3. Does your model stick to your clothes? How does this help you understand how seeds stick to animals?

Draw Conclusions

How is the ball a model of a seed that sticks to things?

Watch a Plant Change

Put two plants of the same kind and size by a window. Mark one. Each day, turn the other plant. Do not turn the marked plant. After one week, how has the marked plant changed? Why did it do this?

Review and Test Preparation

Vocabulary Review

Use the best word or words to complete

pollen p. 104

food chain p. 106

1. Powder from flower is _____.

2. A gas that is part of air is _____.

3. A _____ shows how plants and animals are linked by what they eat.

4. A body part or behavior that helps a living thing is an _____.

Check Understanding

5. Name two animals. **Compare** the animals. Tell how the adaptations of these animals are alike and different.

6. Why do animals need plants to breathe?

    A. Plants give off oxygen.

    B. Animals eat plants.

    C. Plants store water.

    D. Animals can hide in plants.

Critical Thinking

7. How do an animal's teeth help you know what it eats? Why?

8. Look at these plants and animals. Draw them in order to show a food chain. Write about what happens.

Chapter

4 Seasons

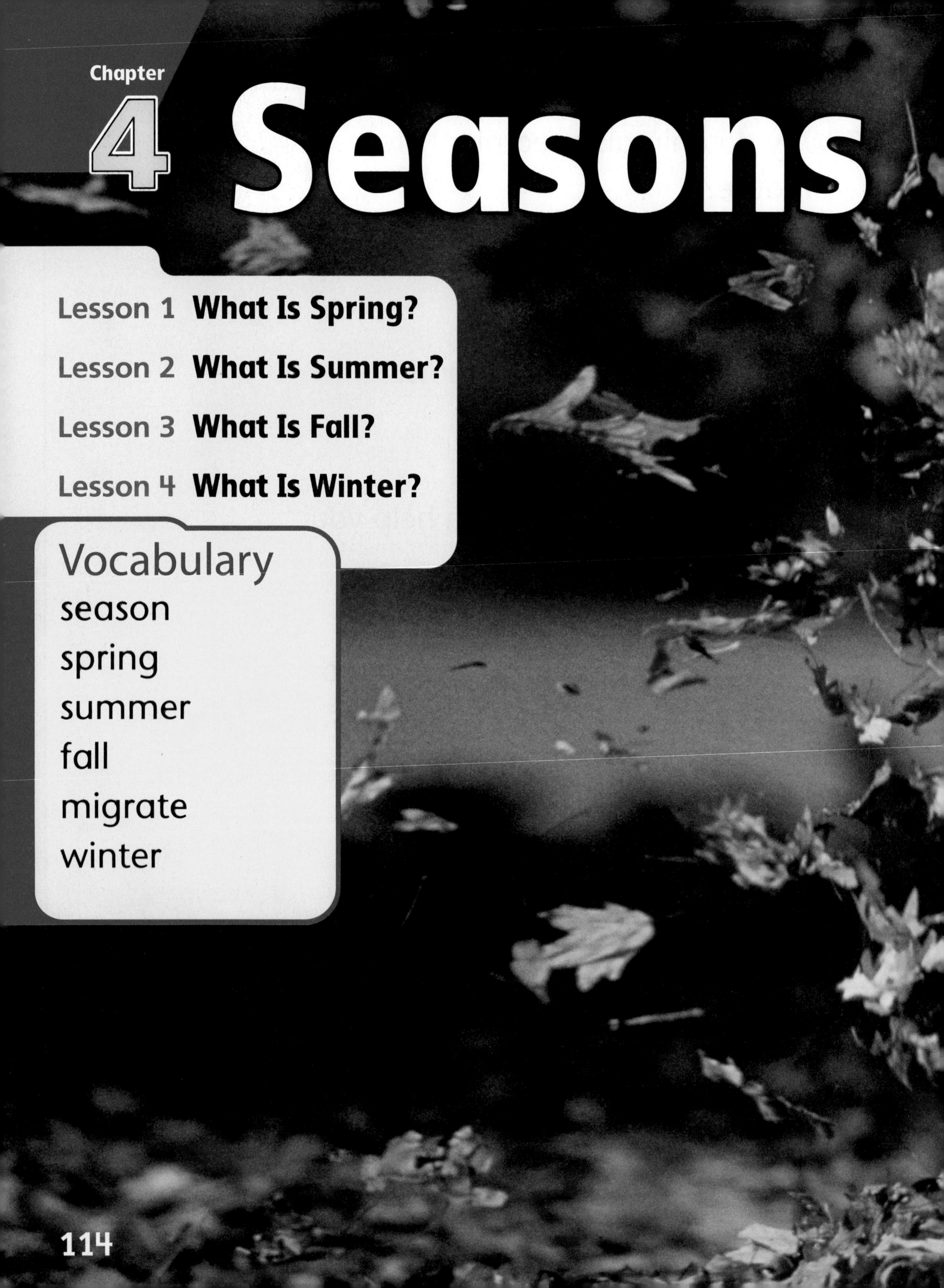

Lesson 1 **What Is Spring?**

Lesson 2 **What Is Summer?**

Lesson 3 **What Is Fall?**

Lesson 4 **What Is Winter?**

Vocabulary

season

spring

summer

fall

migrate

winter

I wonder...

Why do some leaves change color?

What do **you** wonder?

What Is Spring?

Fast Fact

Early spring is the best time to plant a vegetable garden. You can hypothesize about what helps plants grow in spring.

Plants and Light

You need

- **young plant**
- **shoe box with hole**
- **spray bottle**

Step 1

Put the plant in the box.
Put the lid on the box.

Step 2

Place the box so that
the hole faces a window.
Hypothesize about what
will happen to the plant.

Step 3

Spray the plant with
water each day.
After one week, what
happens? Was your
hypothesis correct?

Inquiry Skill

When you **hypothesize**,
you think of an idea.

VOCABULARY
season
spring

READING FOCUS SKILL

MAIN IDEA AND DETAILS Look for the main ideas about spring.

Seasons

A **season** is a time of year. A year has four seasons. The seasons are spring, summer, fall, and winter. They form a pattern. After every winter comes spring.

Science Up Close

Seasons

March

Sunday	Monday	Tuesday	Wednesday	Thursday	Friday	Saturday
	1	2	3	4	5	6
8	9	10	11	12	13	
14	15	16	17	18	19	20
21	22	23	24	25	26	27
28	29	30	31			

Spring starts in the month of March.

118

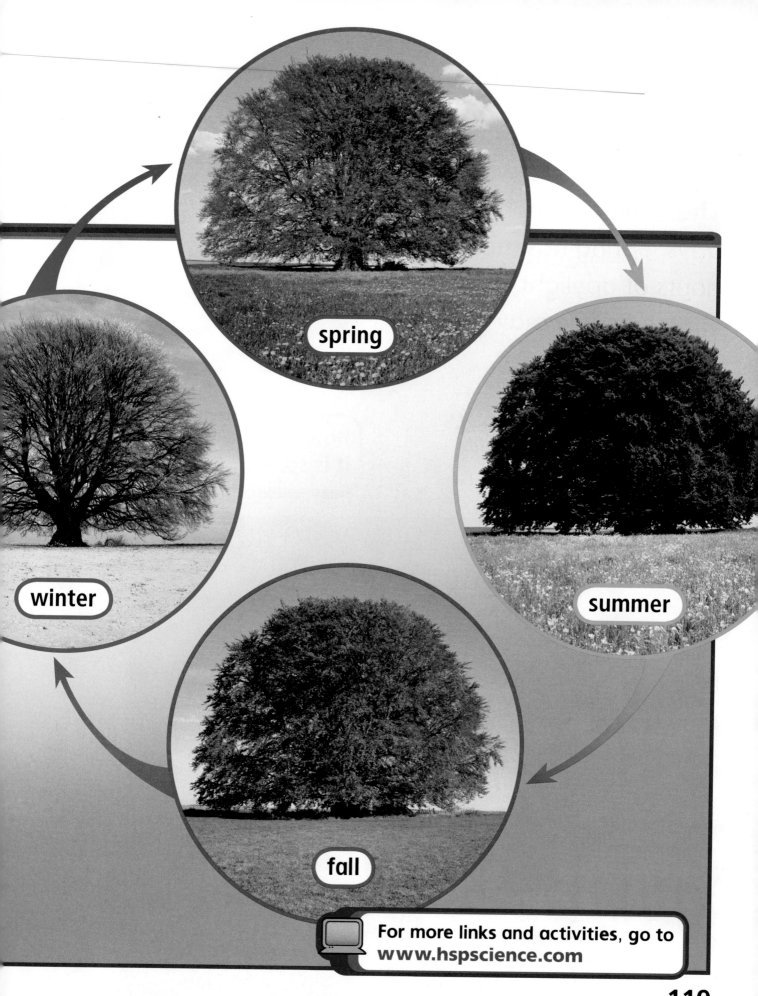

spring

summer

fall

winter

For more links and activities, go to
www.hspscience.com

Spring

Spring is the season after winter. In spring, the weather gets warmer. There may be many rainy days. Spring has more hours of daylight than winter. People may go outside more.

rain

 MAIN IDEA AND DETAILS
What is the weather like in spring?

How can you tell it is spring?

Plants in Spring

Many plants begin to grow in spring. They get more warmth, light, and rain in spring than in winter. Plants may grow new leaves and flowers.

MAIN IDEA AND DETAILS
Why do many plants grow well in spring?

flowers

flowering tree

121

Animals in Spring

Spring is a good time for many animals to have their young. New plants are food for the young. Some young animals are born live. Others hatch from eggs. It is easy for them all to find food.

MAIN IDEA AND DETAILS

Why is spring a good time for animals to have their young?

geese and goslings

ewe and lambs

122

Focus Skill

1. MAIN IDEA AND DETAILS Copy and complete this chart.

Spring

Main Idea
Spring is one of the four seasons.

detail
The weather gets **A** _____ in spring.

detail
There are more hours of **B** _____.

detail
Many plants begin to **C** _____.

detail
Many animals have their **D** _____.

2. SUMMARIZE Use the chart to write a lesson summary.

3. VOCABULARY Tell about the **season** in this picture.

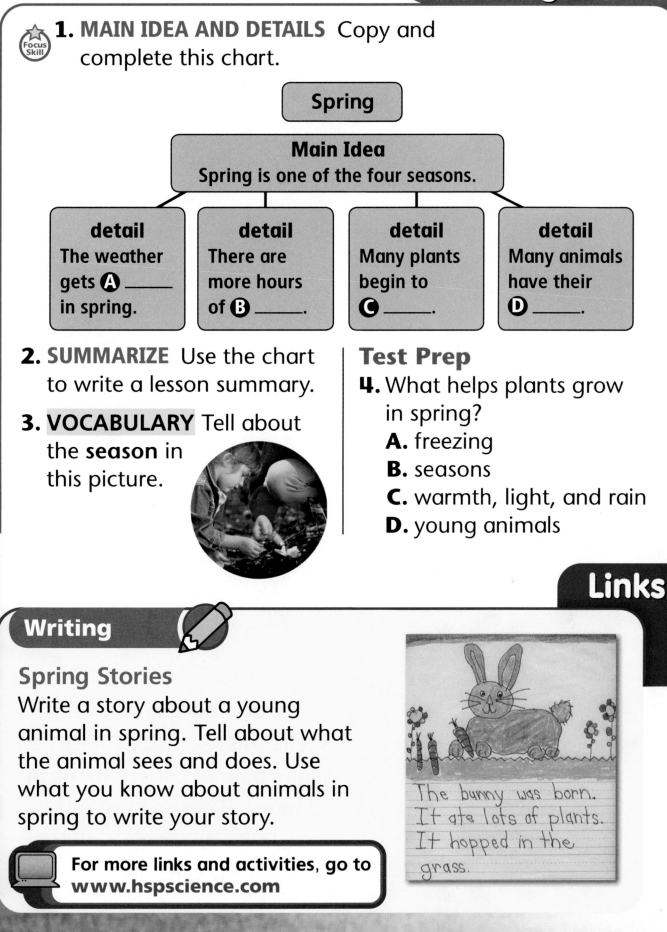

Test Prep

4. What helps plants grow in spring?
- **A.** freezing
- **B.** seasons
- **C.** warmth, light, and rain
- **D.** young animals

Links

Writing

Spring Stories
Write a story about a young animal in spring. Tell about what the animal sees and does. Use what you know about animals in spring to write your story.

For more links and activities, go to www.hspscience.com

The bunny was born. It ate lots of plants. It hopped in the grass.

What Is Summer?

Fast Fact

There are more kinds of shells than you can count. Many people collect shells in summer. You can infer why people do different activities in different seasons.

Hot-Weather Activities

You need

- **seasons picture cards**

Work with a partner. Talk about what people do in summer.

Look at each card. Find clues that tell about the season. **Infer** which pictures show summer.

Compare your ideas with your classmates' ideas. How do you know which pictures show summer?

Inquiry Skill

To **infer**, you use what you already know to figure out something.

Reading in Science

VOCABULARY

summer

READING FOCUS SKILL

MAIN IDEA AND DETAILS Look for the main ideas about summer.

Summer

Summer is the season after spring. Like spring, it has many hours of daylight. Summer weather can be hot. People wear light clothes. Some places may have thunderstorms.

 MAIN IDEA AND DETAILS
What is summer?

hot weather

How can you tell it is summer?

Plants in Summer

Summer weather helps many plants grow. Trees have many green leaves. Some plants grow fruits.

MAIN IDEA AND DETAILS
How can plants change in summer?

tomato plant

tree with leaves

127

Animals in Summer

Animals have ways to stay cool in summer. Some cool off in mud or water. Others lose fur so that their coats are lighter.

In summer, young animals can find plants and other food. They grow bigger.

pig cooling off in mud

MAIN IDEA AND DETAILS
Focus Skill
What is one way animals stay cool in summer?

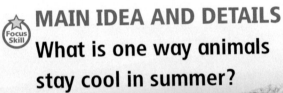

bison shedding fur

Focus Skill

1. MAIN IDEA AND DETAILS Copy and complete this chart.

Summer

Main Idea
Summer is the season after spring.

detail
The weather can be **A** _____.

detail
Some plants grow **B** _____.

detail
Animals have ways to stay **C** _____.

2. DRAW CONCLUSIONS Why do some people like cold drinks in summer?

3. VOCABULARY Use the word **summer** to tell about the picture.

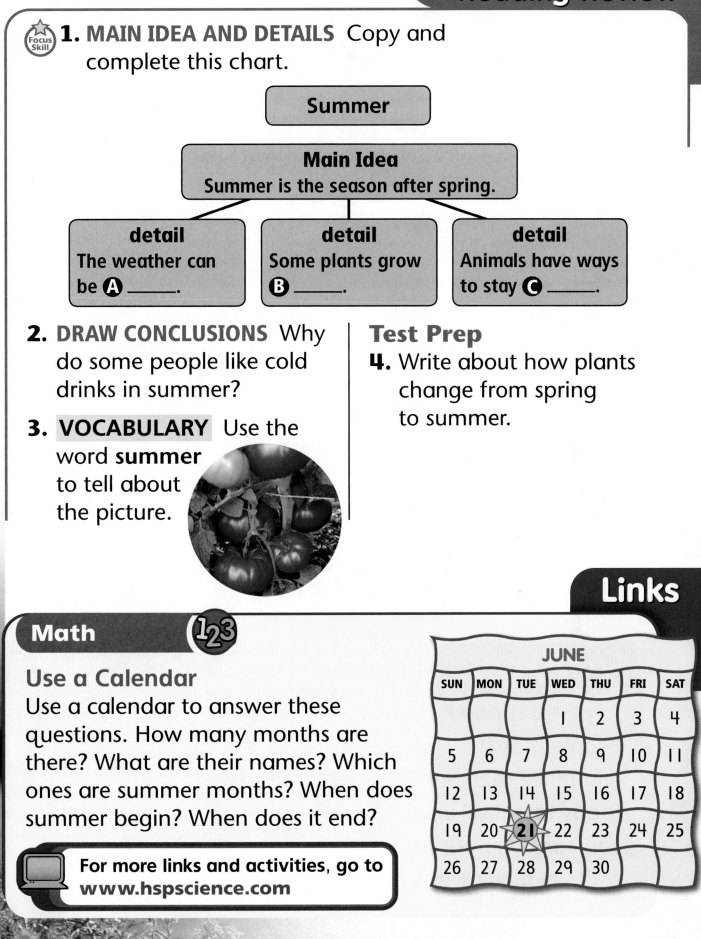

Test Prep

4. Write about how plants change from spring to summer.

Links

Math 123

Use a Calendar
Use a calendar to answer these questions. How many months are there? What are their names? Which ones are summer months? When does summer begin? When does it end?

For more links and activities, go to www.hspscience.com

JUNE						
SUN	MON	TUE	WED	THU	FRI	SAT
			1	2	3	4
5	6	7	8	9	10	11
12	13	14	15	16	17	18
19	20	21	22	23	24	25
26	27	28	29	30		

What Is Fall?

Fast Fact

Apples get ripe in fall. People pick the apples and make them into foods to eat all year. You can compare fruits in many ways.

Compare Seeds

You need

- **fruits with seeds**

- **hand lens**

Step 1

Look at the fruits with the hand lens. Find the seeds. **Compare** the seeds. How are they alike? How are they different?

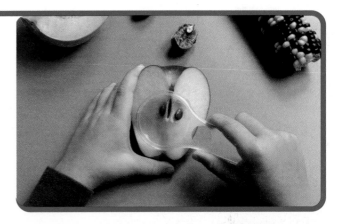

Step 2

Draw and label pictures of the fruits and seeds.

Step 3

Talk about how the seeds are alike. Then talk about how they are different.

Inquiry Skill

Look at the sizes, shapes, and colors of the seeds to **compare** them.

Reading in Science

VOCABULARY
fall
migrate

(Focus Skill) **READING FOCUS SKILL**
CAUSE AND EFFECT Look for reasons that plants and animals change in fall.

Fall

Fall is the season after summer. It has fewer hours of daylight than summer. The temperature gets cooler. People wear heavier clothes.

(Focus Skill) **CAUSE AND EFFECT** Why do people wear heavier clothes in fall?

How can you tell it is fall?

cleaning up leaves

Plants in Fall

In many places, leaves of some trees change color and then fall. This happens because they do not get as much daylight as in summer.

Some fruits get ripe in fall. Then they are ready to pick and eat.

CAUSE AND EFFECT Why do we pick some fruits in fall?

Insta-Lab

Swim!

Why do many people swim outdoors in summer and not in fall? Put a cup of water under a lamp. **CAUTION:** The lamp may be hot! Put another cup of water in a shady place. Which cup of water warms up faster?

squashes

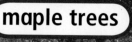

maple trees

Animals in Fall

As the air gets cooler, food may be harder for animals to find. Some animals store food to eat later. Others **migrate**, or move to new places, to find food.

squirrel carrying food

 CAUSE AND EFFECT

Why do some animals store food in fall?

geese migrating

134

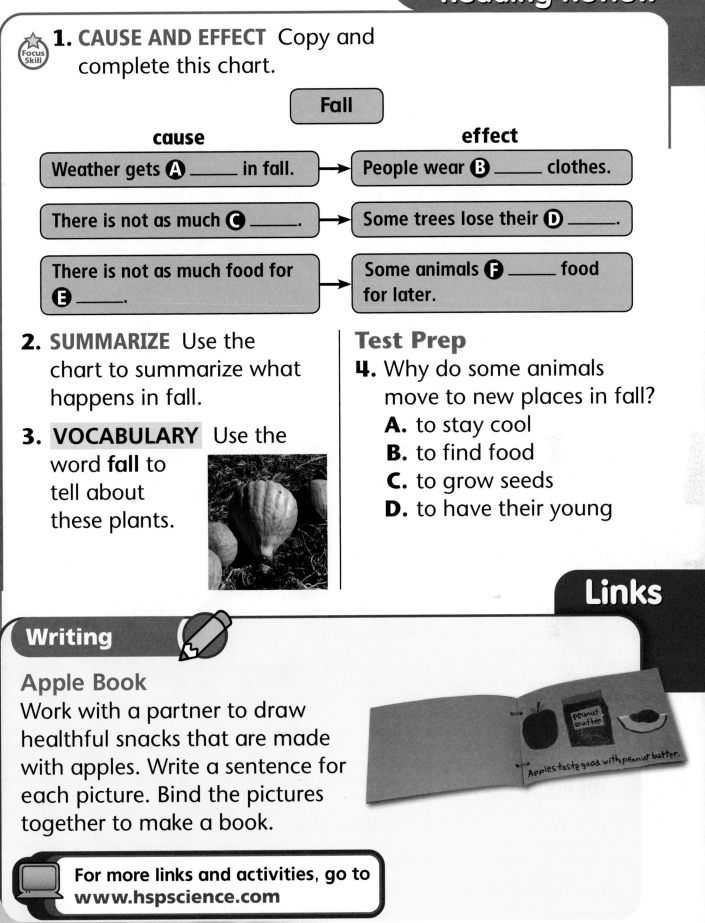

1. CAUSE AND EFFECT Copy and complete this chart.

Fall

cause	effect
Weather gets **A** _____ in fall.	People wear **B** _____ clothes.
There is not as much **C** _____.	Some trees lose their **D** _____.
There is not as much food for **E** _____.	Some animals **F** _____ food for later.

2. SUMMARIZE Use the chart to summarize what happens in fall.

3. VOCABULARY Use the word **fall** to tell about these plants.

Test Prep

4. Why do some animals move to new places in fall?
  A. to stay cool
  B. to find food
  C. to grow seeds
  D. to have their young

Links

Writing

Apple Book
Work with a partner to draw healthful snacks that are made with apples. Write a sentence for each picture. Bind the pictures together to make a book.

peanut butter

Apples taste good with peanut butter.

For more links and activities, go to **www.hspscience.com**

What Is Winter?

Fast Fact

Some trees stay green all year, even in winter. Draw conclusions about what happens to plants and animals in winter.

How to Stay Warm

You need

- plastic bag
- ice water
- mitten

Step 1

Work in a small group. Put your hand in the bag. Dip the bag into the water. How does your hand feel?

Step 2

Put on the mitten. Put your hand in the bag, and dip the bag into the water. How does your hand feel?

Step 3

Draw a conclusion about what can keep you warm in winter. Tell what you found out.

Inquiry Skill

To **draw conclusions**, use what you observed to decide why something happens.

VOCABULARY
winter

 READING FOCUS SKILL

MAIN IDEA AND DETAILS Look for the main ideas about winter.

Winter

Winter is the season after fall. Winter has fewer hours of daylight than any other season. In some places, the air is cold. Snow may fall. People in these places wear very heavy clothes. In other places, the air may just get cooler.

How can you tell it is winter?

 MAIN IDEA AND DETAILS How is winter different from fall?

138

Plants in Winter

Many plants have no leaves in winter. Other plants stay green.

Some plants rest. They do not grow until it gets warm again. Other plants die.

 MAIN IDEA AND DETAILS
What can happen to plants in winter?

holly

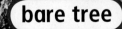
bare tree

Animals in Winter

Food can be hard to find in winter. Some animals eat food that they stored in fall. Others sleep until spring.

Some animals change color to stay safe. Some grow thick coats to stay warm.

(Focus Skill) MAIN IDEA AND DETAILS How do some animals change in winter?

This animal changes color in winter.

This animal grows a thick coat in winter.

Focus Skill

1. **MAIN IDEA AND DETAILS** Copy and complete this chart.

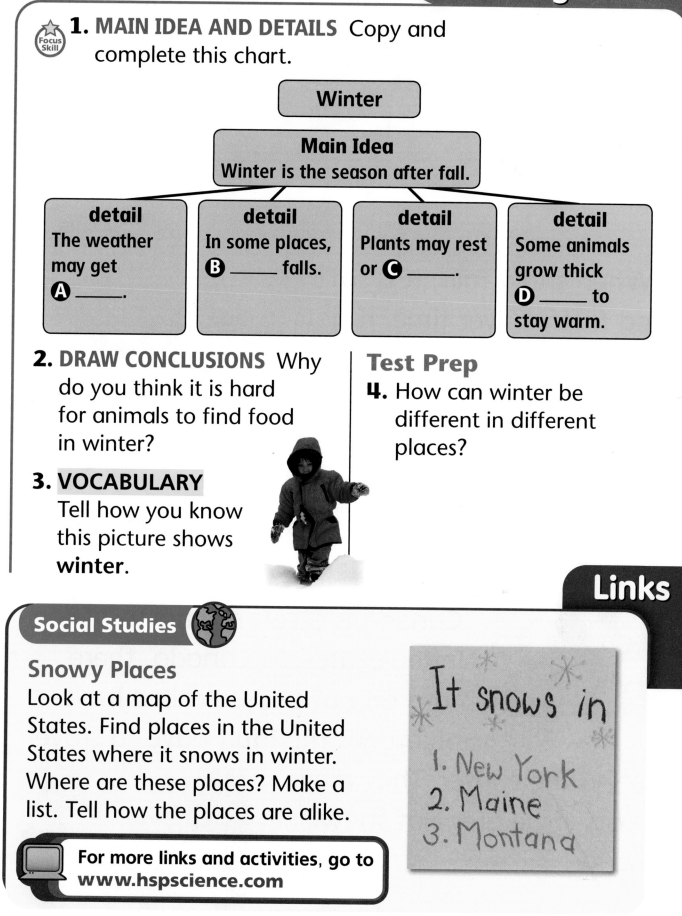

Winter

Main Idea
Winter is the season after fall.

detail
The weather may get **A** ____.

detail
In some places, **B** ____ falls.

detail
Plants may rest or **C** ____.

detail
Some animals grow thick **D** ____ to stay warm.

2. **DRAW CONCLUSIONS** Why do you think it is hard for animals to find food in winter?

3. **VOCABULARY** Tell how you know this picture shows winter.

Test Prep
4. How can winter be different in different places?

Links

Social Studies

Snowy Places
Look at a map of the United States. Find places in the United States where it snows in winter. Where are these places? Make a list. Tell how the places are alike.

For more links and activities, go to www.hspscience.com

It snows in
1. New York
2. Maine
3. Montana

Snow Is Useful

When snow falls, it is soft and fluffy. Over time, it gets packed down.

Snow is strong and holds heat well. Some people use it to build homes. These homes are called igloos.

The Inuit

Canada is a country north of the United States. In Canada, there is a group of people called Inuit. Sometimes the Inuit have to travel during the winter. They move across large areas of snow and ice.

To use a tent on the snow and ice would be too cold. So the Inuit use snow to build an igloo.

The Inuit cut snow into blocks. Then they stack the blocks into a curved shape. It looks sort of like the top of your head. A narrow tunnel is built. It is used to get into the igloo. The tunnel stops the wind from blowing in.

- The largest known snowflake was almost a foot across.
- No two snowflakes are alike.
- All snowflakes have six sides.
- Stampede Pass, Washington, is the snow capital of the United States!

THINK ABOUT IT

Why do you think igloos are built only during the winter?

Find out more! Log on to
www.hspscience.com

Meet Ivy the Inventor

During fall and winter, it gets dark outside earlier. That means that things like mailboxes may be hard to see. Ivy Lumpkin came up with an idea to help people see mailboxes better.

Ivy put two nightlights into a clear tube. The lights run on batteries. Then she put a mailbox on top of the tube. When it is dark out, the nightlights shine and people can see the post. Bright idea, Ivy!

Cool Colors

What to Do

1. Put a thermometer inside each T-shirt.

2. Put the T-shirts in a sunny place. Record the temperature in each.

3. Wait one hour. Record the temperatures. Which colors stayed cooler? Which color got the warmest?

Materials
- 3 thermometers
- 3 T-shirts

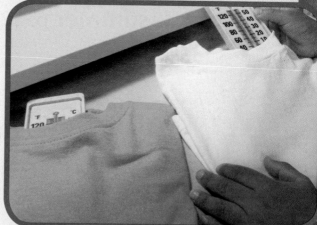

Draw Conclusions
What kinds of colors will help you stay cool?

Favorite Seasons

Take a survey. Find out which season the most people in your class like best. Make a bar graph to show what you learn. Share your graph with your classmates.

Review and Test Preparation

Vocabulary Review

Match the word to its picture.

1. spring p. 120

3. fall p. 132

2. summer p. 126

4. winter p. 138

A.

C.

B.

D.

Check Understanding

5. What is a season? Tell **details** about one season.

Focus Skill

6. In which season would you see trees with many green leaves? Tell why.

7. Why do some animals shed some of their fur in summer?

  A. to stay warm

  B. to hide

  C. to find food

  D. to stay cool

Critical Thinking

8. Tell how the tree changes with each season.

Cleveland MetroParks Zoo

The Cleveland MetroParks Zoo opened in 1882. It had only 14 deer. The deer came from the area.

In 1955, people from the zoo went to Africa. They brought back 10 animals. There were three elephants, two hippos, two rhinos, and three giraffes.

Today, you can see many animals. They come from all over the world.

Today, most new zoo animals are born in zoos.

In the wild, some animals are in danger. Zoos take some of these animals and care for them. At the zoo, the animals get everything they need. Zoos take special care of the animals' young. They work to keep many kinds of animals alive.

Wolves are endangered. The Cleveland MetroParks Zoo is working to keep them alive.

Think and Do

1. **SCIENCE AND TECHNOLOGY** Where do you live? Why do you need a home? Where do wild animals live? Draw a picture of a wild animal and its home.

2. **SCIENTIFIC THINKING** Work with a partner. Choose an animal that lives at the Cleveland MetroParks Zoo. Find out as much as you can about it. Draw pictures to tell what you learned. Share your work.

LS-1 Explore organisms' basic needs; **SI-5** Draw conclusions; **SI-8** Communicate work; **SK-3** Everyone can do science

149

Hale Farm

Columbus

Hale Farm

Going to Hale Farm is like going back in time. How? Hale Farm is just like it was more than 150 years ago.

Farmers today use big machines to help them. At Hale Farm, the work is done with small tools. Animals help with some of the work.

building at Hale Farm

Ohio has four seasons. They are spring, summer, fall, and winter.

Spring is the time for planting. In summer, the growing plants need care.

Farmers harvest crops in early fall. In winter, the ground is left to rest. It will be ready for new plants in spring.

farmers and working farm animals

Who eats the food grown on a farm?

Think and Do

I. SCIENCE AND TECHNOLOGY What do plants need to grow? Make a list or draw a picture.

2. SCIENTIFIC THINKING Think about the seasons in Ohio. How does a plant grow in each season? Draw four pictures of a tree. Show how the tree looks in each season.

 LS-2 Explain where food comes from; **LS-4** Investigate animal/plant interactions; **LS-5** Recognize influence of seasons; **ST-6** Explore need for tools

The Biggest Buckeye Tree

Buckeye trees are big. Most grow to be 60 feet tall.

The biggest buckeye tree is in Huron County, Ohio. It is 77 feet tall. That's taller than a 6-story building!

buckeye tree

Buckeye trees grow best near streams. They also grow well on low land. Ohio has a lot of both. That's why buckeye trees grow so well here.

The biggest trees grow in open spaces. They can grow bigger when other trees do not crowd them.

One kind of buckeye tree always has five leaves on each stem.

These little buckeyes might grow into big trees.

Think and Do

1. **SCIENCE AND TECHNOLOGY** How do you get food and water into your body? How does a plant get food and water? Draw a picture.

2. **SCIENTIFIC THINKING** Find pictures of outdoor plants—one that lives near water and one that lives in a desert or in the hills. Talk to a friend about how they are different.

Compare Growth

Materials
- books about plants and animals
- paper
- ruler
- markers

What to Do
1. Draw a line across a sheet of paper. Make marks on the line to show the years of your life. Number them.
2. Draw a picture at each mark. Show how tall you were at that age.
3. Make a chart to show how a buckeye tree grows.
4. Compare the charts.

Draw Conclusions
1. Which grows faster, you or the tree?
2. Which will grow taller?

Nature Scavenger Hunt

Materials
- pencil
- paper

What to Do
1. Copy the chart.
2. Go outside. Take the chart and a pencil with you.
3. Look for plants and animals that match the words on the chart.
4. Draw pictures in the boxes to show what you find.

is red	is green	is black	is brown
is something animals eat		lives in a tree	has four legs

Draw Conclusions
1. Can plants and animals share a place to live?
2. How do animals use plants?
3. Could anyone do this activity?

SI-1 Infer/Predict; **SI-7** Estimate; **SI-8** Communicate work; **SI-9** Describe and compare accurately; **SK-2** Demonstrate good explanations

155

Physical Sciences

The chapters and features in this unit address these Grade Level Indicators from the Ohio Academic Content Standards for Science.

Chapter 5 Changes in Matter

PS-1   Classify objects according to the materials they are made of and their physical properties.

PS-2   Investigate that water can change from liquid to solid or solid to liquid.

PS-3   Explore and observe that things can be done to materials to change their properties (e.g., heating, freezing, mixing, cutting, wetting, dissolving, bending and exposing to light).

PS-4   Explore changes that greatly change the properties of an object (e.g., burning paper) and changes that leave the properties largely unchanged (e.g., tearing paper).

Chapter 6 Motion

PS-5   Explore the effects some objects have on others even when the two objects might not touch (e.g., magnets).

PS-6   Investigate a variety of ways to make things move and what causes them to change speed, direction and/or stop.

Chapter 7 Energy

PS-7   Explore how energy makes things work (e.g., batteries in a toy and electricity turning fan blades).

PS-8   Recognize that the sun is an energy source that warms the land, air and water.

PS-9   Describe that energy can be obtained from many sources in many ways (e.g., food, gasoline, electricity or batteries).

Unit C Ohio Expeditions

The investigations and experiences in this unit also address many of the Grade Level Indicators for standards in Science and Technology, Scientific Inquiry, and Scientific Ways of Knowing.

TO: beninohio@hspscience.com
FROM: marcus@hspscience2.com
RE: National Inventors Hall of Fame

Dear Ben,

We went to the National Inventors Hall of Fame in Akron today. I learned a lot about inventors. Remember that bed-maker we wanted to invent? I have some ideas for it now.

Your pal,
Marcus

Experiment!

Gravity As you do this unit, you will learn about how things move. Plan and do a test. Find out how to make a toy truck go farther.

5 Changes in Matter

Vocabulary

matter	water vapor
property	condensation
mass	burning
mixture	
evaporation	

I wonder...

Why do things filled with air float in water?

What do **YOU** wonder?

How Can We Classify Matter?

Fast Fact

Ice is solid matter. It has a shape. This ice is shaped like an old car. You can compare the shapes of objects.

160

Kinds of Matter

You need

● **jar of water**   ● **zip-top bag filled with air**   ● **block**

Shake the water in the jar. How does it change?

Press the air in the bag. How does it change?

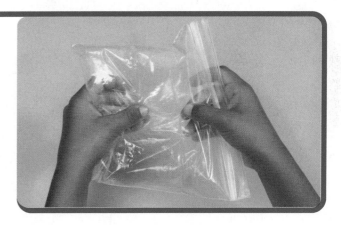

Turn the block. Squeeze it. How does it change? **Compare** the changes to the water, the air, and the block.

Inquiry Skill

When you **compare** things, it helps you see how they are alike and how they are different.

VOCABULARY

matter
property
mass

READING FOCUS SKILL

COMPARE AND CONTRAST Look for ways matter can be alike and different.

Forms of Matter

Matter is what all things are made of. Everything around you is matter. Trees, water, and air are matter. You are matter, too.

What things in this picture are made of matter?

Matter can be a solid, a liquid, or a gas. The hills are solids. The water is a liquid. The air in the balloons is a gas.

COMPARE AND CONTRAST How are the objects in this picture alike? How are they different?

Properties of Matter

Matter has properties. A **property** is one part of what something is like.

All matter has two main properties. Matter takes up space. It also has mass. **Mass** is the amount of matter in an object.

What are some properties of these objects?

Matter has other properties. Color, size, and shape are properties of matter. The material something is made of is also a property.

COMPARE AND CONTRAST
Compare the materials these objects are made of. How are they different?

Insta-Lab

A Matter of Space

Choose three objects. Put them in order from the one that takes up the least space to the one that takes up the most space. Tell why you ordered the objects the way you did.

Measuring Mass

You can use a balance to find the mass of a solid. Look at the objects on this balance. Does the shell have the same mass as the two weights? How do you know?

 COMPARE AND CONTRAST Does a person have more or less mass than this shell?

balance

Focus Skill

1. COMPARE AND CONTRAST Copy and complete this chart.

Matter

alike

All matter takes up **Ⓐ** _____.

All matter has **Ⓑ** _____.

different

Matter can be a solid, a **Ⓒ** _____, or a **Ⓓ** _____.

2. SUMMARIZE Use the chart to summarize the lesson.

3. VOCABULARY Tell about the block by naming some of its **properties**.

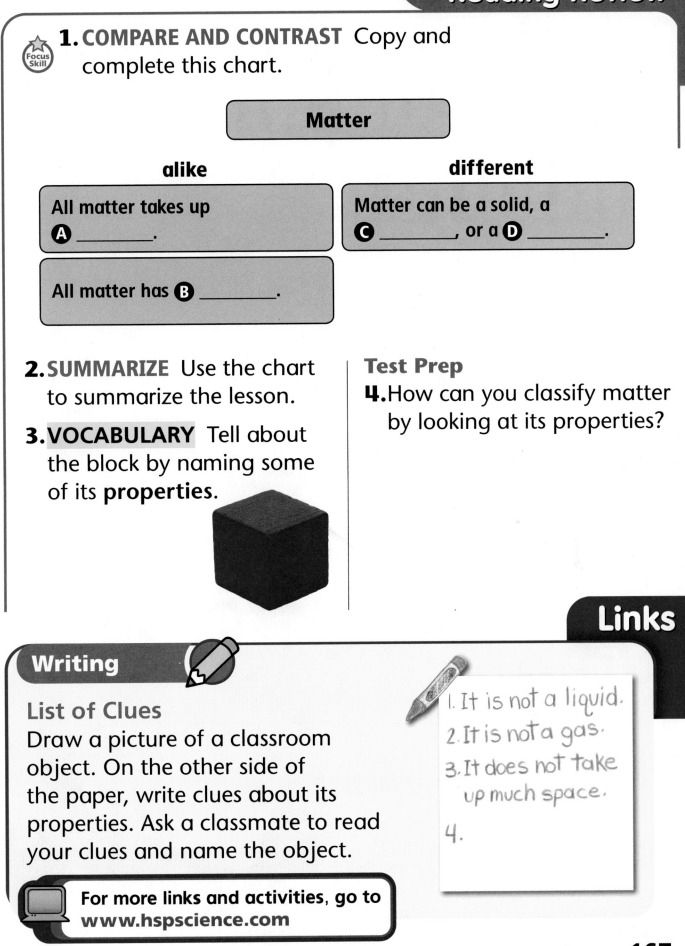

Test Prep

4. How can you classify matter by looking at its properties?

Links

Writing

List of Clues
Draw a picture of a classroom object. On the other side of the paper, write clues about its properties. Ask a classmate to read your clues and name the object.

1. It is not a liquid.
2. It is not a gas.
3. It does not take up much space.

4.

For more links and activities, go to www.hspscience.com

How Can Matter Change?

Fast Fact

These children are making mixtures. You can communicate about foods you like when you make tasty mixtures.

Make a Mixture

You need

- dried fruits and seeds • measuring cup • zip-top bag

Step 1

Measure the same amounts of fruits and seeds. Use the measuring cup.

Step 2

Put the foods in the bag. Close the bag and shake it.

Step 3

What changed? What stayed the same? **Communicate** what you see.

Inquiry Skill

When you **communicate** you share with others what you have observed.

VOCABULARY
mixture

READING FOCUS SKILL

CAUSE AND EFFECT Look for ways matter can change. Find the cause for each change.

Mixing Matter

When you mix matter, you make a **mixture**. Solids, liquids, and gases can all be parts of mixtures. Things you put into a mixture do not change.

Fruit salad is a mixture. Each piece of fruit in the mixture does not change.

fruit salad

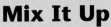
lemonade

Lemonade is a mixture. It has water, lemon juice, and sugar. The sugar is a solid. You mix it with the two liquids. You no longer see the sugar, but it is there.

CAUSE AND EFFECT What is one way you can tell the sugar in the lemonade is still there?

Insta-Lab

Mix It Up

Mix four spoonfuls of cornstarch with two spoonfuls of water. Roll the mixture in your hands. Pour it from hand to hand. What happens? Tell about the cornstarch and water before and after you mixed them.

Kinds of Changes

You can change matter when you cut it. Cutting or tearing changes its size and shape. Look at other ways to change matter.

 CAUSE AND EFFECT How does matter change when you cut it?

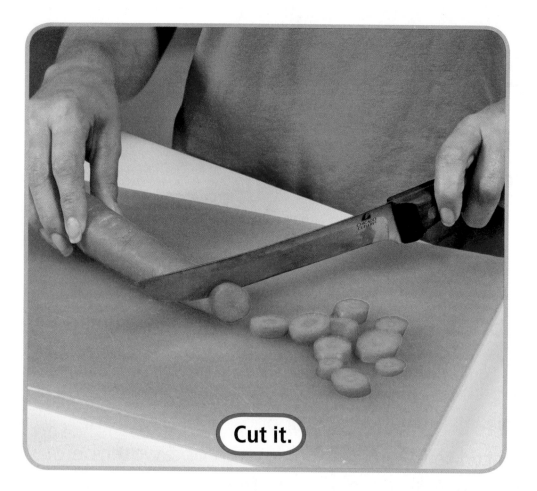

Break it.

Cut it.

Shape it.

Tear it.

Slice it.

173

Measuring Matter

When you change just the shape of matter, its mass stays the same.

Look at the cheese on the balance. Both sides were once the same. Then the block on the right was cut into cubes. Its mass did not change.

CAUSE AND EFFECT How does the balance show that the mass of the cheese is the same?

block of cheese

cheese cubes

Focus Skill

1. CAUSE AND EFFECT Copy and complete this chart.

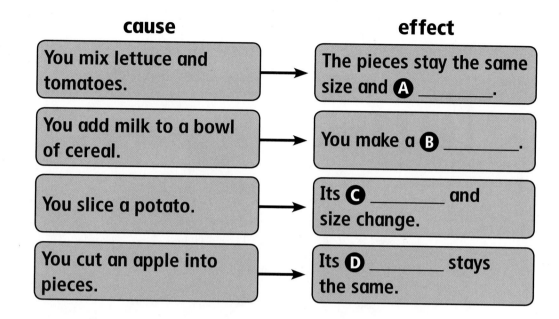

cause	effect
You mix lettuce and tomatoes.	The pieces stay the same size and **A** _____ .
You add milk to a bowl of cereal.	You make a **B** _____ .
You slice a potato.	Its **C** _____ and size change.
You cut an apple into pieces.	Its **D** _____ stays the same.

2. SUMMARIZE Use the chart to summarize this lesson.

3. VOCABULARY Use the word **mixture** to tell about the picture.

Test Prep

4. When the shape of matter is changed, what stays the same?

Links

Writing

Snack Recipe

Make up a healthful snack that is a mixture of different foods. Write your recipe. List what you need. Write the steps to tell how to make it. Share your recipe with your classmates.

Margie's Munchy Mix

What you need

1 cup pumpkin seeds
1 cup raisins
cereal

For more links and activities, go to www.hspscience.com

How Can Water Change?

Fast Fact

Water can be solid, liquid, or gas. You can predict what the solid ice in the pond will become when it gets warmer.

176

Freezing

You need

- **plastic tub with lid**
- **water**
- **marker**

Step 1

Fill a plastic tub halfway with water. Mark the water level on the side of the tub.

Step 2

Put a lid on the tub. Place the tub in the freezer. **Predict** what will happen to the water.

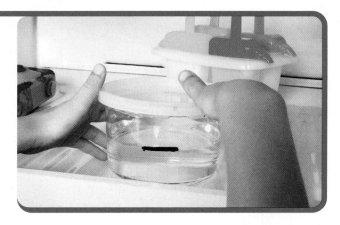

Step 3

Wait one day. How did the water and the tub change?

Inquiry Skill
When you **predict**, you tell what you think will happen.

 PS-2 Investigate how water changes, **PS-3** Explore changes in properties, **PS-4** Explore physical and chemical changes, **SI-1** Infer/Predict

177

Reading in Science

PS-2 Investigate how water changes, **PS-3** Explore changes in properties, **PS-4** Explore physical and chemical changes

VOCABULARY

evaporation
water vapor
condensation

(Focus Skill) **READING FOCUS SKILL**

CAUSE AND EFFECT Look for what causes water to change into a solid, liquid, and gas.

Freezing

Water can be solid, liquid, or gas. It changes forms when enough heat is added or taken away.

Liquid water may freeze. It becomes ice. Ice is solid water. Water freezes when enough heat is taken away.

liquid

The juice in the tray is mostly water. How will it change when it freezes?

The juice has changed to a solid. It is now an ice pop.

liquid

⭐ **CAUSE AND EFFECT** What caused the juice to change from a liquid to a solid?

solid

melting

Melting

The ice pop is melting. Warm air is adding heat. When enough heat is added, ice melts. It changes from a solid to a liquid.

CAUSE AND EFFECT What caused the ice pop to melt?

Insta-Lab

Which Melts Faster?

Set out two plates. Put one ice cube on each plate. Place a lamp over just one plate. **CAUTION:** The lamp may be hot! Wait five minutes. Which ice cube melted more? Why?

Evaporation

The water in this pot is changing to a gas. Liquid water changes when enough heat is added. This change is called **evaporation**. Water as a gas is called **water vapor**. You can not see water vapor. It is in the air.

Focus Skill **CAUSE AND EFFECT** What causes water to change to a gas?

condensation

Condensation

Air near this cold glass has water vapor. The cold takes away heat from air. This changes the water vapor into liquid water. The water drops collect on the outside of the glass. This change from gas to liquid is called **condensation**.

 CAUSE AND EFFECT What caused water drops to form on the outside of the glass?

Focus Skill

1. CAUSE AND EFFECT Copy and complete this chart.

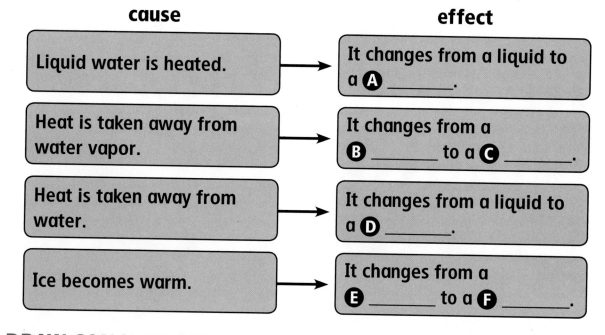

cause	effect
Liquid water is heated.	It changes from a liquid to a **A** _____ .
Heat is taken away from water vapor.	It changes from a **B** _____ to a **C** _____ .
Heat is taken away from water.	It changes from a liquid to a **D** _____ .
Ice becomes warm.	It changes from a **E** _____ to a **F** _____ .

2. DRAW CONCLUSIONS Can ice that has melted change back to a solid? Explain.

3. VOCABULARY Use the words **water vapor** and **condensation** to tell about this picture.

Test Prep

4. How can you change water to a gas?

   A. Take heat away.

   B. Freeze it.

   C. Add heat.

   D. Melt it.

Links

Math

Measure and Compare

Use a thermometer to find the temperature of a glass of water. Then find the temperature of a bowl of ice. Compare. Which one has the lower temperature?

For more links and activities, go to
www.hspscience.com

What Are Some Other Changes to Matter?

Fast Fact

Fire is so hot that it can change one kind of matter into another. Drawing conclusions can help you figure out why matter changes.

How Matter Can Change

You need

- **black plastic bowl**
- **foil**
- **gelatin**

Step 1

Place the foil, shiny side up, in the bowl.

Step 2

Put the gelatin on the foil in the bowl. Put the bowl in a sunny spot. Wait one hour.

Step 3

Observe the gelatin. **Draw conclusions** from what you observed. Explain.

Inquiry Skill

Use your observations and what you know to **draw conclusions**.

VOCABULARY

burning

 READING FOCUS SKILL

CAUSE AND EFFECT Look for the causes and effects of burning and cooking.

Burning and Cooking

Fire and cooking change matter into new matter. This new matter can not turn back into what it was before.

The fire is burning this wood. **Burning** changes it. It becomes ashes and smoke. They can not turn back into wood.

Cooking heats food. The heat changes a marshmallow. It turns from white to brown. It can not turn back to white.

CAUSE AND EFFECT How and why does a marshmallow change when it is cooked?

Focus Skill

Insta-Lab

Uncooked and Cooked

How does uncooked pasta look? How does cooked pasta look? Draw pictures to show this. How did the pasta change? Tell a classmate.

Making Muffins

1. **Mix the ingredients.**

2. **Pour the mixture into a pan.**

3. **Bake the mixture.**

   What changes do you see? Why?

For more links and activities, go to www.hspscience.com

188

1. CAUSE AND EFFECT Copy and complete this chart.

cause	effect
Fire burns wood.	→ The wood changes into **A** _____ matter. The wood becomes ashes and **B** _____.
Fire cooks a marshmallow.	→ The marshmallow's **C** _____ changes.

2. SUMMARIZE Write a summary of this lesson.

3. VOCABULARY Use the word **burning** to tell about this picture.

Test Prep

4. What happens when paper burns?
   A. Its shape stays the same.
   B. Its size stays the same.
   C. Its matter stays the same.
   D. Its matter changes.

Links

Art

Before and After
Draw pictures of a food before and after it is cooked. Write about each picture. Tell about the food's texture, size, color, shape, and taste. Share your work with your class.

Dough

Bread

For more links and activities, go to www.hspscience.com

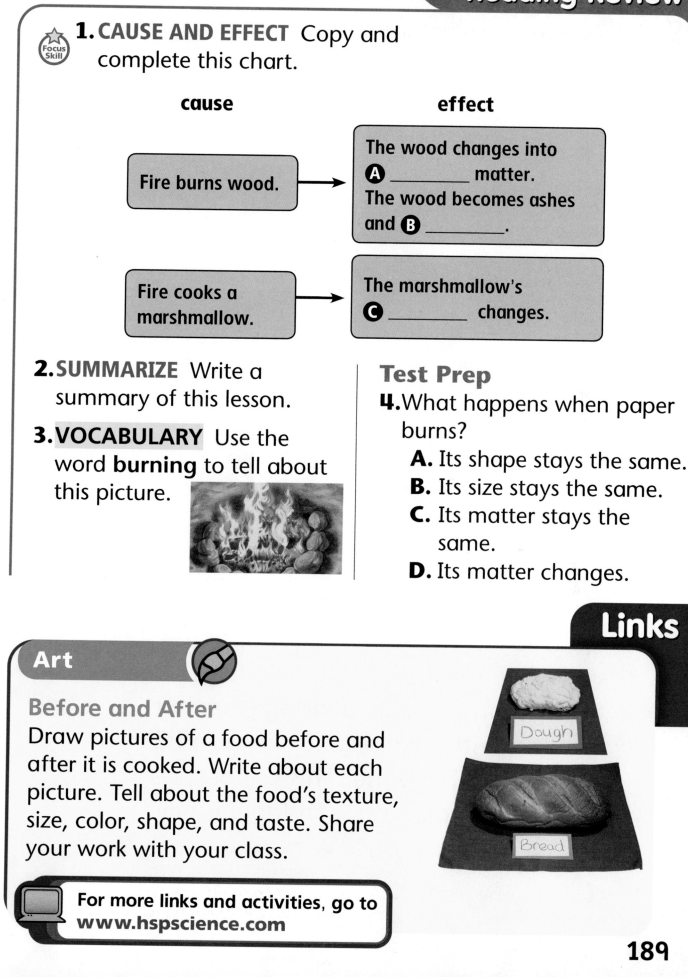

The Future of Bandages

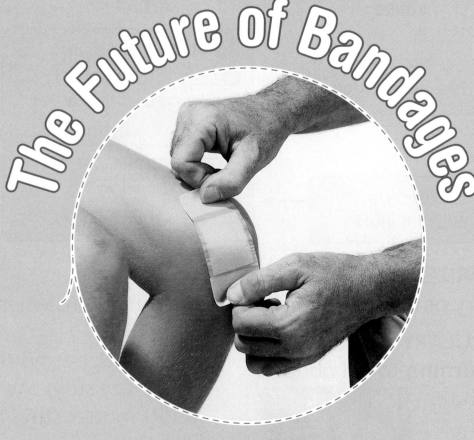

All kids get scrapes and cuts. When you get a scrape or a cut, you put a plastic bandage on. What happens when it is time to change that bandage? Ouch! Pulling off a plastic bandage can hurt.

Scientists have recently invented a new fabric bandage. This bandage is better than a plastic bandage. It never has to be taken off!

The New Bandage in Town

The new bandage works like the body's own bandage—a scab. After a cut covered with the new bandage has healed, the body absorbs the fibers. The bandage simply disappears.

Tiny Strands

The new bandage is made up of thousands of tiny hair-like strands. The strands are also found in a person's blood. The strands found in a person's blood act like a net across a cut to stop bleeding.

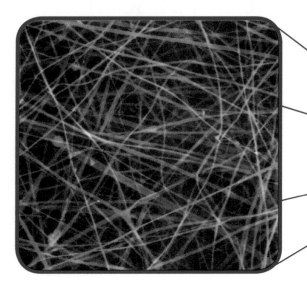

Think About It

How does the new bandage change as a cut heals?

Find out more! Log on to
www.hspscience.com

A Famous Scientist

Everyone can do science! Everyone can invent things! Albert Einstein is one of the most famous scientists. Einstein loved math and science.

As he grew up, Einstein read a lot. He wanted to learn more about the things around him. He thought about things he could see. He thought about things that were much too small to see. He used his imagination to look at things in new ways. He thought about matter in ways that no one ever had before.

Mixing Matter

What to Do

1. Put a spoonful of salt into the warm water. Stir well.
2. Pour the mixture of salt and water into the pan.
3. Put the pan in a warm spot. Predict what will happen.
4. Wait two days. Then observe. Was your prediction correct?

You need
- $\frac{1}{2}$ cup warm water
- spoon
- pie pan
- salt

Draw Conclusions

What happened to the water? What was left in the pan? What does this show about mixtures?

Heat Changes Food

Place a cracker, an ice cube, some chocolate chips, and some butter on separate pieces of foil. Put them under a hot light.
CAUTION: Lamp may be hot! Check every five minutes. What changes do you see?

Review and Test Preparation

Vocabulary Review

Use the words to complete the sentences.

matter p. 162   **mixture** p. 170

property p. 164   **water vapor** p. 181

1. What all things are made of is called

_____.

2. Water in its gas form is called _____.

3. A mix of two or more things is a _____.

4. One part of what something is like is called a _____.

Check Understanding

5. What are solids, liquids, and gases?

   A. kinds of matter

   B. shapes

   C. properties

   D. mixtures

Check Understanding

6. What **caused** the bread to change?

F. burning

G. cutting

H. freezing

J. mixing

Critical Thinking

7. What changes would this icicle go through to become water vapor?

8. How does an egg change when it is cooked?

Vocabulary

motion	magnet
speed	attract
force	magnetic force
push	pole
pull	repel
gravity	

I wonder...

What makes a roller coaster move?

What do you wonder?

How Do Things Move?

Fast Fact

The Blue Angels jets move very fast at air shows. They also move in many directions. You can classify objects by the ways they move.

Ways Objects Move

You need

● **objects**

Step 1

Work in a small group.
Move each object.
Observe the way
it moves.

Step 2

Classify the objects by
the ways they move.
Then write about the
groups you made.

Step 3

Talk with classmates
about your groups.
Compare your results.

Inquiry Skill

Classify the objects by
grouping those that move
in the same way.

VOCABULARY
motion
speed

READING FOCUS SKILL

COMPARE AND CONTRAST Look for ways motion and speed are alike and different.

Motion

Things are in motion all around you. When something is in **motion**, it is moving. What is moving here?

jump rope

race car

Objects move at different speeds. **Speed** is how fast something moves. Both of these objects are moving. They are not moving at the same speed. Which is moving faster?

Focus Skill **COMPARE AND CONTRAST** How can speeds of objects be different?

tricycle

Insta-Lab

Motion Graph

Test some toys. Do they move in a straight path, a curved path, a circle, or a zigzag? Record. Then make a bar graph to show how many toys move in each way.

201

How Things Move

Things can move in different ways. An object may move in a straight path. It may move in a curved path. It may move in a circle. It may even move in a zigzag.

zigzag

 Focus Skill

COMPARE AND CONTRAST
What are some different ways an object can move?

curved path

circle

straight path

202

★ Focus Skill **1. COMPARE AND CONTRAST** Copy and complete this chart.

Motion

alike

> All objects in **A** _____ are moving.

different

> The **B** _____ of an object can be fast or slow.

> An object may move in a straight path, in a curved path, in a circle, or in a **C** _____.

2. SUMMARIZE Use the chart to write a summary of this lesson.

3. VOCABULARY Tell about the **motion** in this picture.

Test Prep

4. What are some different ways objects can move?

Links

Writing

Write About Motion
Think of a sport or an active game you like to play. How do you move your body? Write a description. Tell how your body moves when you play.

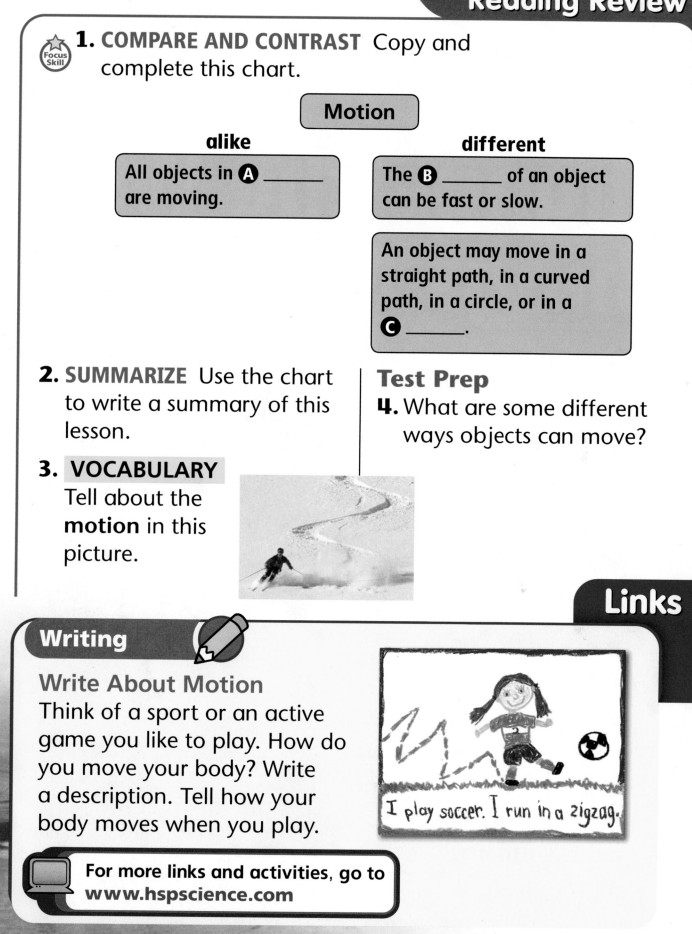

I play soccer. I run in a zigzag.

For more links and activities, go to www.hspscience.com

How Can We Change the Way Things Move?

Fast Fact

A juggler can keep three or more objects in the air at a time. You can plan an investigation to find out ways to make objects move.

Pulling and Pushing Objects

You need

- **small cube**
- **objects to make cube move**

Step 1

How can you use these objects to push or pull the cube? **Plan an investigation** to explore this question.

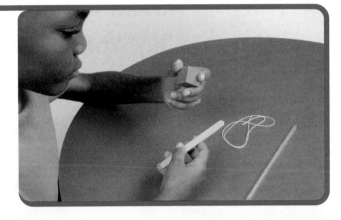

Step 2

Follow your **plan**. Tell how you moved the cube. Use the words **push** and **pull**.

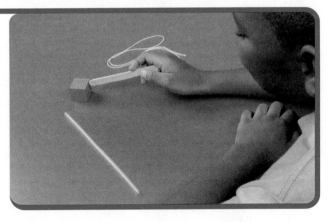

Step 3

Repeat your **plan**. Do you get the same results?

Inquiry Skill

You can **plan an investigation**. Think of ways to move the cube, and then try them.

VOCABULARY	(Focus Skill) **READING FOCUS SKILL**
force	**CAUSE AND EFFECT** Look for actions that cause objects to move.
push	
pull	

Making Things Move

A **force** makes something move or stop moving. You use a force each time you move an object. You use forces to move your body, too.

Pushes and pulls are forces. When you **push** an object, you move it away from you. When you **pull** an object, you move it closer to you.

Focus Skill **CAUSE AND EFFECT** What happens when you push an object?

pulling

pushing

Changing Speed

You use a force to change the speed of an object. These soccer balls are moving very fast. You can use a push to stop a ball. Then you can pull it to you. You can push it away by kicking it to make it move faster.

 CAUSE AND EFFECT What may cause a ball to move faster?

pushing away

pulling to

Changing Direction

You use a force to change an object's direction. When you play baseball, the ball moves to you. Then you hit it with the bat. Hitting the ball is a push. The ball moves away from you.

CAUSE AND EFFECT What happens to a ball when you hit it?

Focus Skill

What force does the boy use to change the ball's direction?

Changing Position

You use a force to change where an object is. You can pull part of a toy truck up and push part of it down. You can push a toy truck into the station and pull it out. You can push it forward and pull it backward.

 CAUSE AND EFFECT How can you change where an object is?

up and down

in and out

forward and backward

1. CAUSE AND EFFECT Copy and complete this chart.

cause   **effects**

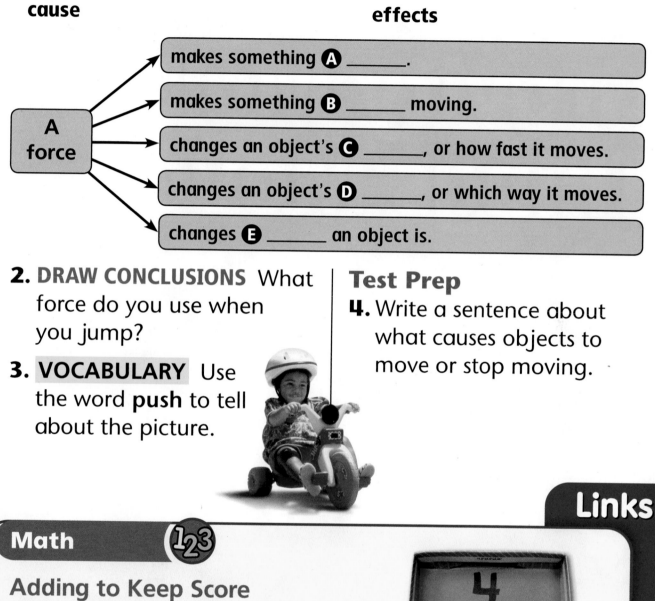

A force

- makes something **A** _____.
- makes something **B** _____ moving.
- changes an object's **C** _____, or how fast it moves.
- changes an object's **D** _____, or which way it moves.
- changes **E** _____ an object is.

2. DRAW CONCLUSIONS What force do you use when you jump?

3. VOCABULARY Use the word **push** to tell about the picture.

Test Prep

4. Write a sentence about what causes objects to move or stop moving.

Links

Math

Adding to Keep Score

In some games, players push objects to score points. Make your own pushing game. Use a box lid. Push a bottle cap from one end to score points. Do this three times. Add your points to find your score.

For more links and activities, go to www.hspscience.com

How Does Gravity Make Things Move?

Gravity pulls your body down a slide. You can predict how gravity will move an object.

How a Ball Will Move

You need

• tape

• ball

• ramp

Step 1

Set up the ramp. **Predict** where the ball will stop when you let it roll down the ramp. Mark the spot with tape.

Step 2

Let the ball roll down the ramp. Do not push it.

Step 3

Was your **prediction** correct? Explain what you found out.

Inquiry Skill

To **predict** how far the ball will go, think about how a ball moves.

(Focus Skill) **READING FOCUS SKILL**

CAUSE AND EFFECT Look for the effect gravity has on objects.

Gravity Makes Things Move

Gravity is a force that pulls things straight down to the ground. It makes things fall unless something is holding them up.

Look at the diver. Nothing is holding her up. Which way will she move? The diver will move down because gravity is pulling her down.

(Focus Skill) **CAUSE AND EFFECT** What effect does gravity have on objects?

diver

dog food

What is gravity moving here?

sled

Insta-Lab

Falling Objects

Watch the way gravity pulls different things down. Your teacher will drop a ball and a pencil together. Observe how they fall and land. Why do you think this happens?

How Things Fall

Gravity moves all objects on Earth the same way. It pulls them straight down. A push or a pull can change an object's path. A push or a pull can hold an object up. If there are no pushes or pulls, all objects fall.

The ball is light. The rock is heavy.

The boy drops the ball and the rock at the same time.

Both fall and land at the same time.

For more links and activities, go to www.hspscience.com

216

Focus Skill

1. CAUSE AND EFFECT Copy and complete this chart.

Gravity

cause

effect

gravity → The object **A** _____ to the ground.

a **B** _____ or a pull on an object → The object's **C** _____ may change.

The object may not fall.

2. SUMMARIE Write two sentences that tell what the lesson is about.

3. VOCABULARY Use the word **gravity** to tell about this picture.

Test Prep

4. How could you stop gravity from pulling a ball to the ground?

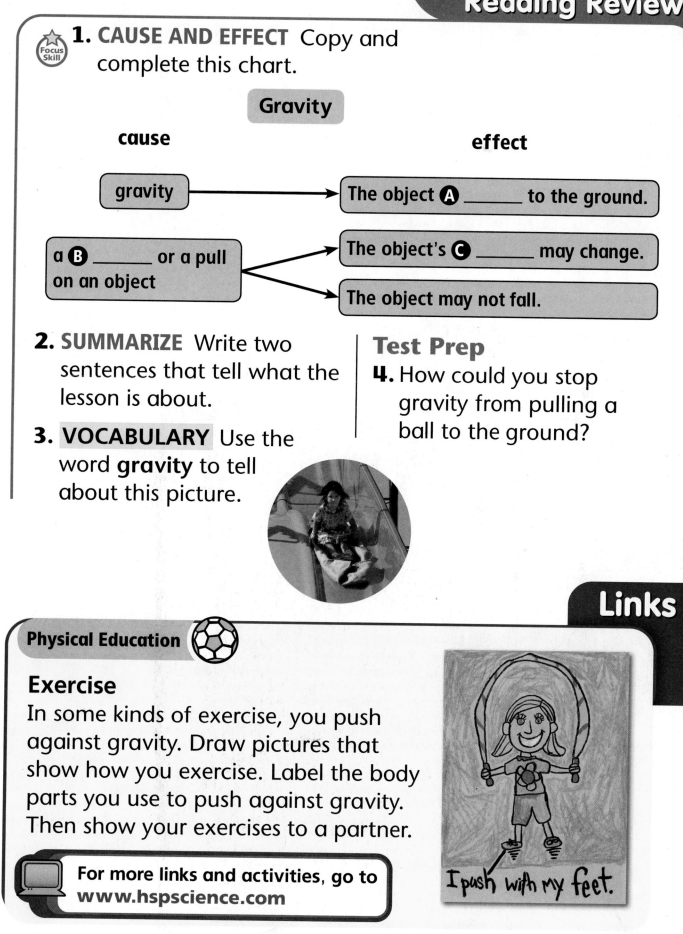

Links

Physical Education

Exercise

In some kinds of exercise, you push against gravity. Draw pictures that show how you exercise. Label the body parts you use to push against gravity. Then show your exercises to a partner.

For more links and activities, go to **www.hspscience.com**

I push with my feet.

How Do Magnets Make Things Move?

Fast Fact

Very strong magnets pick up
heavy loads of recycled steel.
You can hypothesize about
what a magnet will pull.

What Magnets Pull

You need

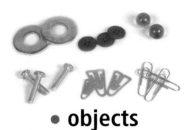

- bar magnet
- objects

Look at the objects.
Which ones will
a magnet pull?
Hypothesize.

Step 2

Test your **hypothesis**.
Use a magnet. Record
your observations.

What a Magnet Can Do		
Object	Pulls	Does Not Pull

Step 3

Was your **hypothesis**
correct? How do
you know?

Inquiry Skill

When you **hypothesize**,
you tell your idea about
something.

Reading in Science

VOCABULARY

magnet   pole
attract   repel
magnetic force

READING FOCUS SKILL

MAIN IDEA AND DETAILS Find out what magnets are and how they move objects.

Magnets

A **magnet** is an object that will **attract**, or pull, things made of iron.

magnets

What does a magnet attract?
You can test objects to see. A magnet
does not attract all metals. It attracts
metals that have iron in them. Steel
has iron in it.

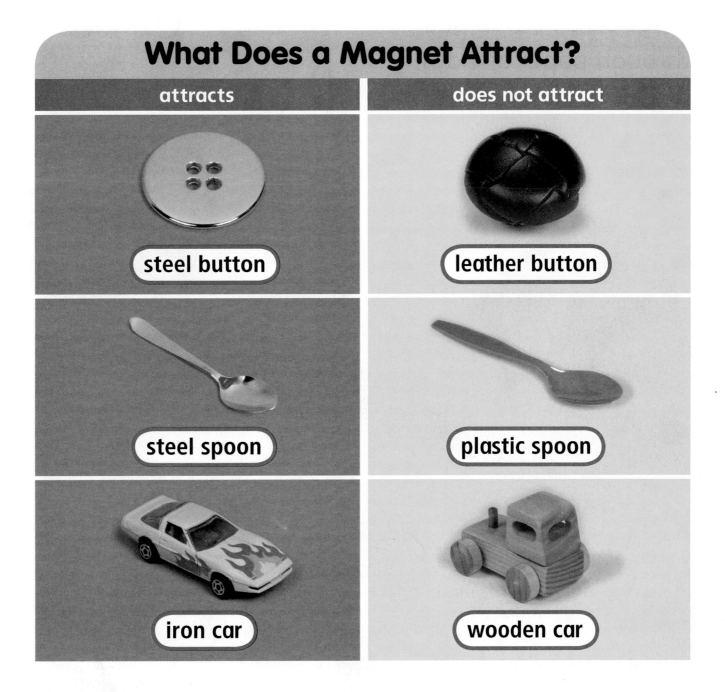

What Does a Magnet Attract?

attracts	does not attract
steel button	leather button
steel spoon	plastic spoon
iron car	wooden car

⭐ **MAIN IDEA AND DETAILS** What is a magnet?

Force of a Magnet

A magnet's pull is called **magnetic force**. Some magnets have a lot of force. They are very strong. Many magnets can even pull through paper or cloth.

magnet pulling through paper

magnet pulling without touching

Magnets attract objects without touching them. Strong ones can pull from far away. This magnet pulls a paper clip on a kite when it is held above it.

⭐ **MAIN IDEA AND DETAILS**
How do you know if a magnet has a strong magnetic force?

Insta-Lab

Move It with a Magnet
Find out what a magnet pulls through. Use a strong magnet. Try to attract a metal clip through paper, cloth, and other materials. Tell what you observe.

Poles of a Magnet

A magnet has an N pole and an S pole. One is at each end of a bar magnet. The **poles** of a magnet are the places where the pull is the strongest.

You can try to put magnets together. Poles that are different will attract each other. Poles that are the same will **repel** each other, or push each other away.

MAIN IDEA AND DETAILS
What are a magnet's poles?

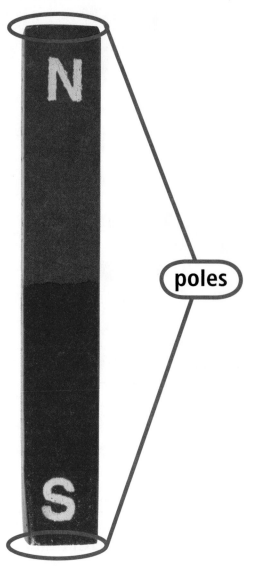

poles

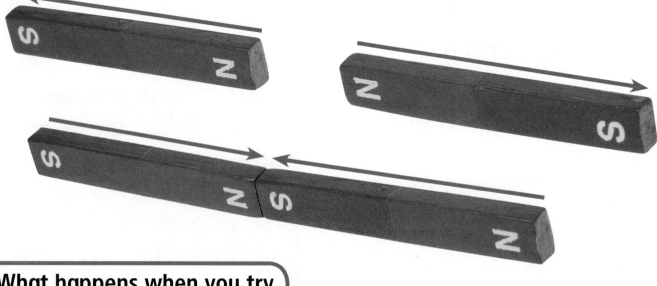

What happens when you try to put magnets together?

Focus Skill

1. MAIN IDEA AND DETAILS Copy and complete this chart.

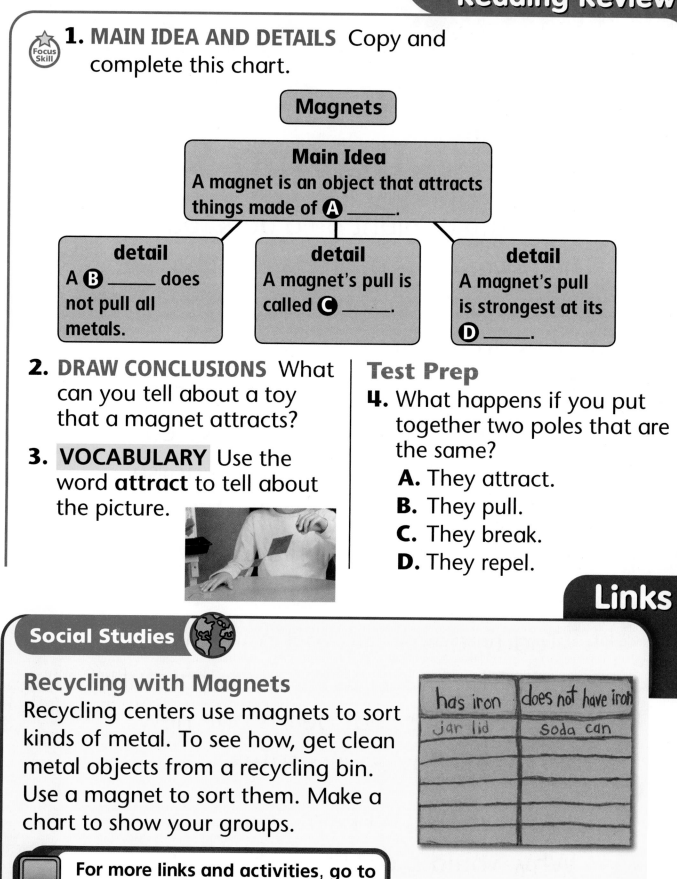

Magnets

Main Idea
A magnet is an object that attracts things made of **Ⓐ** _____.

detail
A **Ⓑ** _____ does not pull all metals.

detail
A magnet's pull is called **Ⓒ** _____.

detail
A magnet's pull is strongest at its **Ⓓ** _____.

2. DRAW CONCLUSIONS What can you tell about a toy that a magnet attracts?

3. VOCABULARY Use the word **attract** to tell about the picture.

Test Prep

4. What happens if you put together two poles that are the same?

A. They attract.

B. They pull.

C. They break.

D. They repel.

Links

Social Studies

Recycling with Magnets
Recycling centers use magnets to sort kinds of metal. To see how, get clean metal objects from a recycling bin. Use a magnet to sort them. Make a chart to show your groups.

has iron	does not have iron
jar lid	soda can

For more links and activities, go to www.hspscience.com

Making Driving Safer

It is late at night on a dark road. The driver of a car starts to fall asleep. Then, snap! The seat belt gets tight. It wakes up the driver!

In the past, people did not worry about falling asleep. They traveled by horse and wagon, and the horse stayed awake! Then cars took the place of wagons. The first cars were slow, but cars got faster over time.

Today, drivers go fast on crowded roads. They need to be more careful than ever. This seat belt is one new tool that keeps drivers safe!

THINK ABOUT IT

Why would a car that goes faster be less safe?

 Find out more! Log on to
www.hspscience.com

Moving with Magnets

John Fowler is learning about magnets. He has learned that a magnet can pick up things that have iron in them.

John took a magnet off the refrigerator at home. He used it to try to pick up things around the house.

John dropped a paper clip in a glass of water. The magnet even pulled the paper clip through the glass and the water!

You Can Do It!

Make a Magnetic Toy

What to Do

1. Cut a small kite from tissue paper.

2. Tie a paper clip to a thread. Tape the clip to the kite. Tape the end of the thread to a table.

3. Hold the magnet above the kite but not touching it. Can you use the magnet to make your kite fly?

Materials

- scissors
- magnet
- tissue paper
- paper clip
- thread
- tape

Draw Conclusions

What part of the kite does the magnet pull? Why?

Wheels Collage

How are a bicycle and skates alike? They have wheels! Some objects could not move without wheels. Draw ten objects with wheels. Use them to make a "Wheels" collage.

Wheels
truck
car

Review and Test Preparation

Vocabulary Review

Choose the word that best completes each sentence.

speed p. 201   **magnet** p. 220

gravity p. 214   **repel** p. 224

1. When magnets push away, they ___.

2. An object that attracts things made of iron is a ___.

3. The force that pulls things to the ground is ___.

4. How fast an object moves is its ___.

Check Understanding

5. Use these pictures to **compare** different ways objects can move.

6. Look at this picture. What is **causing** the sled to move?

　　A. gravity

　　B. magnetic force

　　C. N and S poles

　　D. speed

Critical Thinking

7. Why do you think magnets stick to most refrigerators?

8. List these objects in order from slowest to fastest.

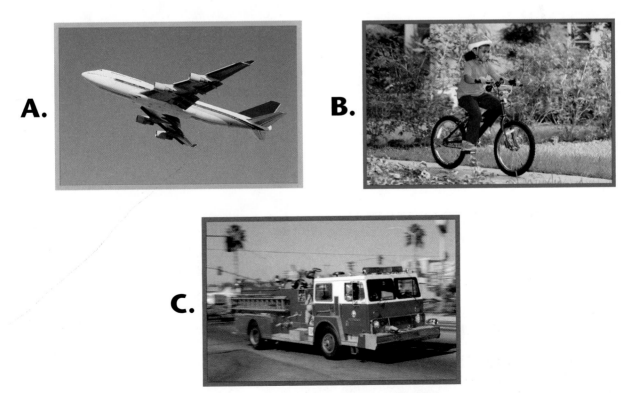

A.

B.

C.

Chapter 7

Energy

Lesson 1 How Does Energy Make Things Work?

Lesson 2 How Can We Conserve Energy?

Lesson 3 Where Do People Get Energy?

Vocabulary

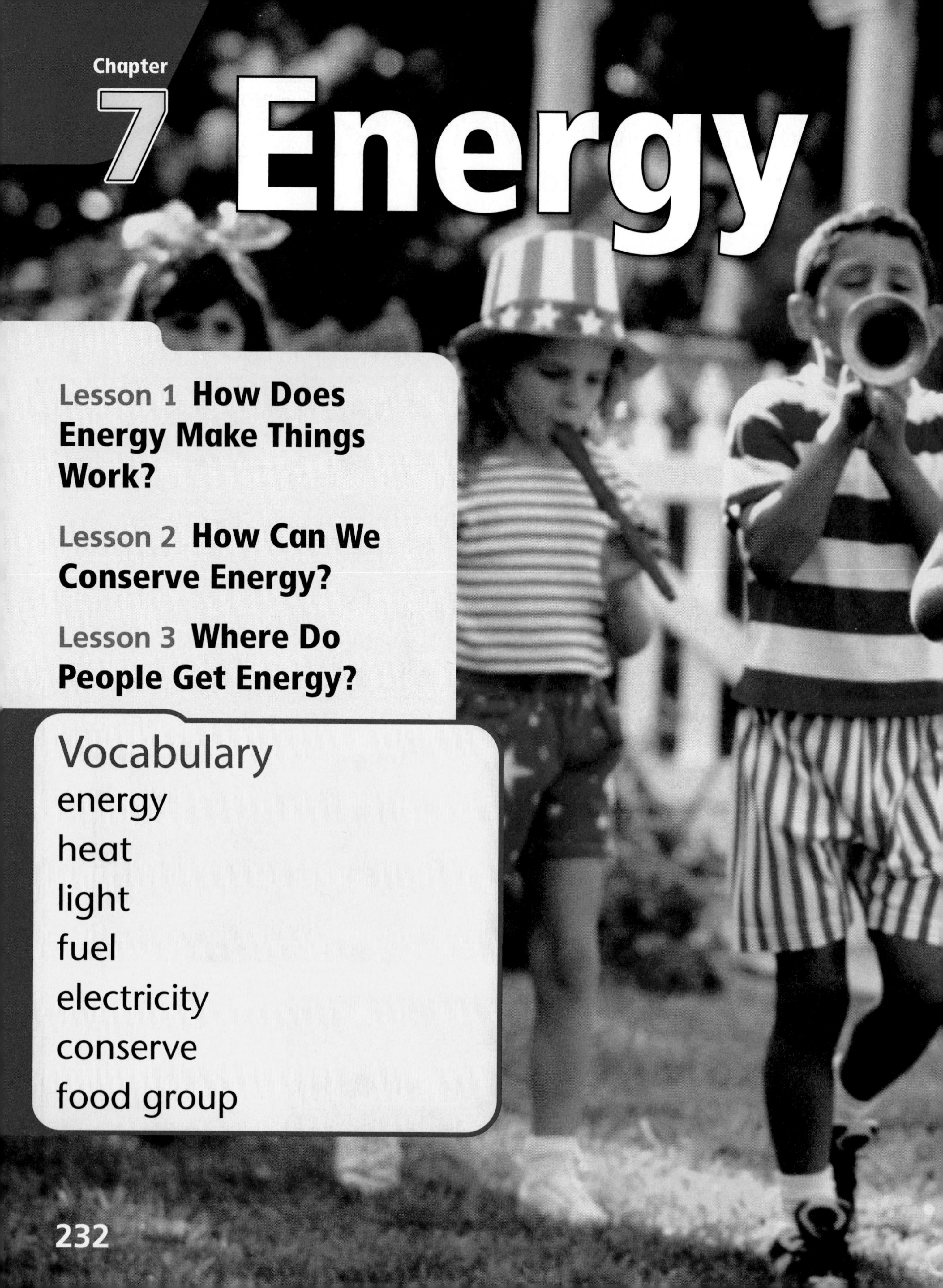

energy
heat
light
fuel
electricity
conserve
food group

I wonder...

Why do musical instruments make different sounds?

What do **you** wonder?

233

How Does Energy Make Things Work?

Fast Fact

Wind turns the blades on a windmill. You can plan an investigation to find out other ways people use wind for energy.

Energy from Wind

You need

- toy car
- clay
- toothpicks
- paper

Step 1

Plan an investigation.
Think of a way to use
the clay, toothpicks, and
paper to make a sail for
the toy car.

Step 2

Carry out the **plan** you
made in Step 1.

Step 3

Blow on the sail. Observe
what happens. Then
communicate what
made the car move.

Inquiry Skill
**You decide how to
experiment when you
plan an investigation.**

VOCABULARY

energy
heat
light
fuel
electricity

READING FOCUS SKILL

MAIN IDEA AND DETAILS Look for details about the forms of energy and about where energy comes from.

Energy

Energy causes matter to move or change. Energy has different forms.

Heat is energy that makes things warmer. People use heat to warm their homes and cook their food.

Heat makes water boil.

Light is energy that lets you see. The sun gives off light during the day. Fires and electric lights give off light, too.

Sound is energy that you can hear. You hear sound when it travels to your ears.

 MAIN IDEA AND DETAILS What are some forms of energy?

You can hear a lion's roar.

Electric lights light this city.

237

Where Energy Comes From

Most energy on Earth comes from the sun. The sun gives off heat that warms land, water, and air. Plants use sunlight to make food. People and animals eat the plants to get energy.

sun

Energy also comes from wind and moving water. They can make things move by pushing on them. How do wind and water move the kiteboard?

Energy from some energy stations comes from water.

kiteboarding

natural gas burner

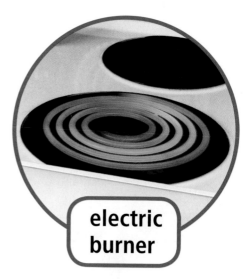

electric burner

gasoline pump

Energy also comes from fuels. **Fuel** is something burned for energy. Some fuels are wood, coal, and oil. Gasoline and natural gas are fuels, too. Most cars burn gasoline to move. Some people use natural gas for heating and cooking.

MAIN IDEA AND DETAILS
Where does energy come from?

Insta-Lab

Water Power
Place three small objects in the middle of a pan. Pour some water into the pan at one end. Observe what happens to the objects.

239

Electricity

Electricity is a form of energy. It runs many things you use each day. These things change electricity into other forms of energy. A lamp changes electricity into light and heat.

outlet

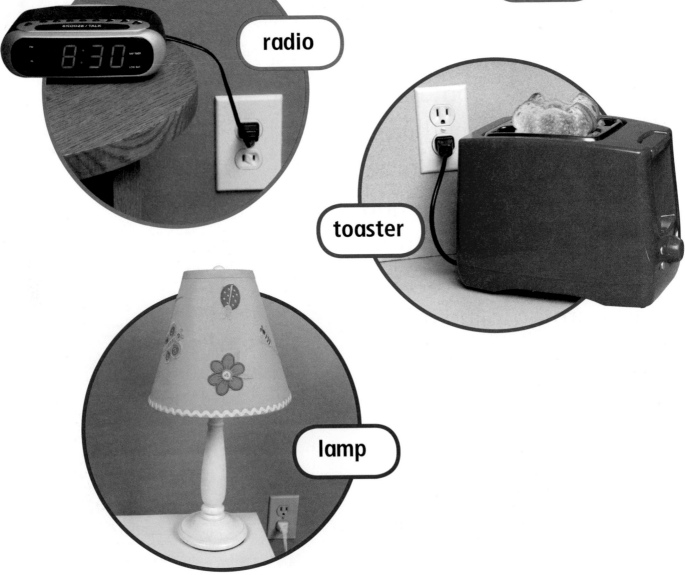

radio

toaster

lamp

These things need electricity to work. They get electricity from batteries. A battery stores energy and changes it into electricity.

 MAIN IDEA AND DETAILS What kinds of energy can electricity be changed into?

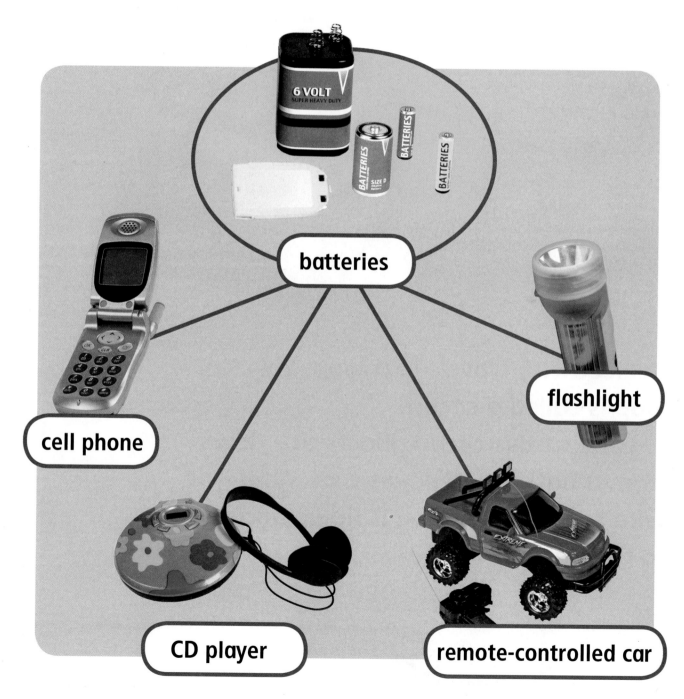

batteries

cell phone

flashlight

CD player

remote-controlled car

Circuits

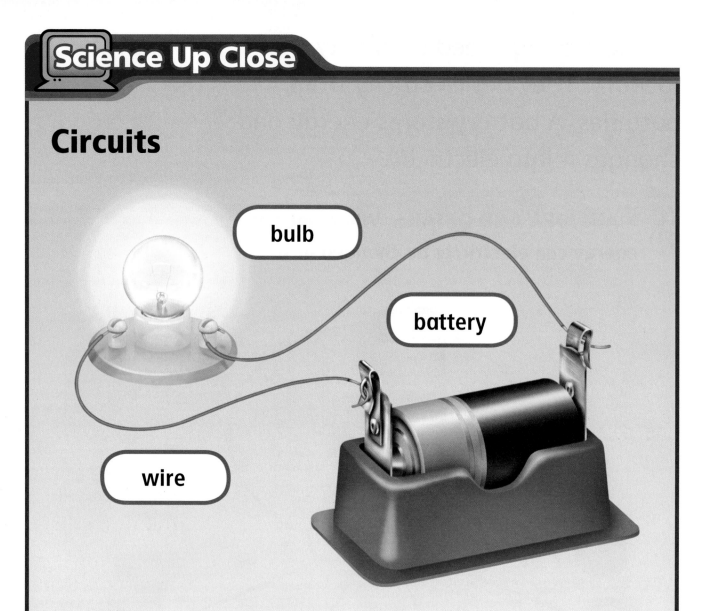

bulb

battery

wire

Electricity travels in a loop. This loop is called a circuit.

Look at this circuit. Electricity flows from a battery. It moves through a wire to the bulb. Then it flows back to the battery.

For more links and activities, go to
www.hspscience.com

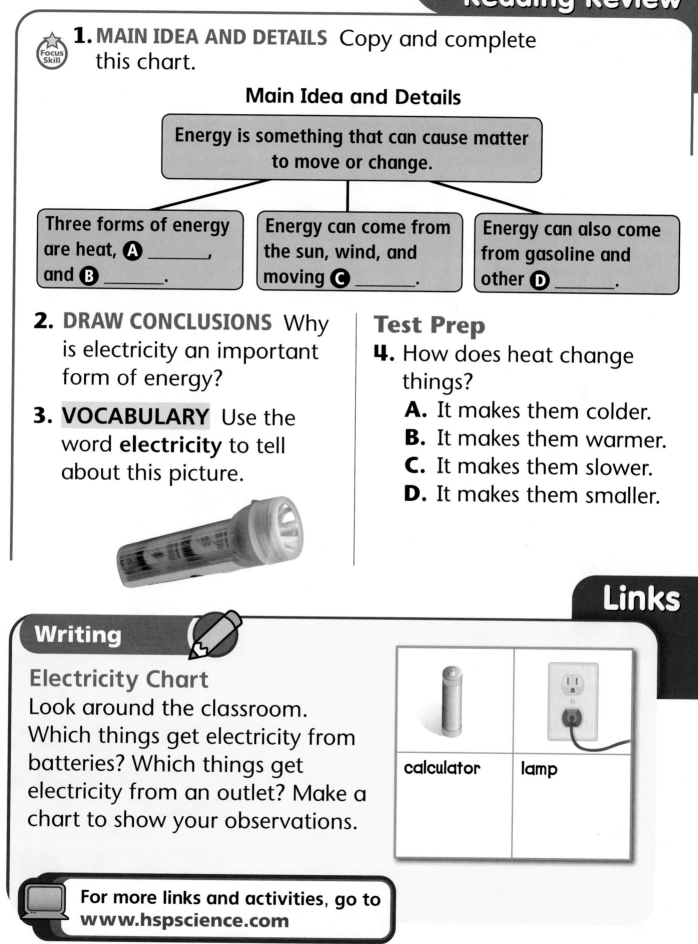

1. **MAIN IDEA AND DETAILS** Copy and complete this chart.

Main Idea and Details

Energy is something that can cause matter to move or change.

Three forms of energy are heat, **A** _____, and **B** _____.	Energy can come from the sun, wind, and moving **C** _____.	Energy can also come from gasoline and other **D** _____.

2. **DRAW CONCLUSIONS** Why is electricity an important form of energy?

3. **VOCABULARY** Use the word **electricity** to tell about this picture.

Test Prep

4. How does heat change things?
   A. It makes them colder.
   B. It makes them warmer.
   C. It makes them slower.
   D. It makes them smaller.

Links

Writing

Electricity Chart
Look around the classroom. Which things get electricity from batteries? Which things get electricity from an outlet? Make a chart to show your observations.

calculator	lamp

For more links and activities, go to
www.hspscience.com

How Can We Conserve Energy?

Fast Fact

You can use heat from the sun to dry clothes. You can plan an investigation to find out how the sun warms Earth.

Heat from the Sun

You need

- cup of soil

- 2 thermometers

Does the sun warm soil faster than it warms air? **Plan an investigation** to find out. Write your **plan**.

Follow your **plan** to **investigate** your ideas.

Share with the class what you learned.

Inquiry Skill

You **plan an investigation by** thinking of ideas and trying them out.

Reading in Science

(Focus Skill) READING FOCUS SKILL

MAIN IDEA AND DETAILS Look for the main idea about conserving energy and the details that tell more about it.

Conserving Energy

To **conserve** energy, you use it carefully. You use only what you need and do not waste it. This helps make sure everyone will have enough energy for the future.

(Focus Skill) MAIN IDEA AND DETAILS Why is conserving energy important?

Which person is conserving energy?

Conserving Fuel

Conserving fuel is a way to save energy. Gasoline makes cars go. You conserve gasoline when you bike.

Natural gas helps heat many homes. You conserve natural gas when you turn down the heat.

MAIN IDEA AND DETAILS

Focus Skill

What are two ways people can conserve fuel?

Bike to Save

Make a list of all the places you can bike to. Then make a plan. Tell how you can save gasoline by biking more often. Be sure to go over your plan with parents or adult family members.

biking

turning down the heat

Conserving Electricity

Another way to save energy is to conserve electricity. You can turn off lights when you are not using them. You can turn off toys and other things that use batteries.

turning off the light

⭐ (Focus Skill) **MAIN IDEA AND DETAILS** How can you conserve electricity?

turning off a toy car

Focus Skill

1. MAIN IDEA AND DETAILS Copy and complete this chart.

Main Idea
When you **Ⓐ** _____ energy, you use it carefully.

details
You conserve **Ⓑ** _____ when you bike.
You conserve natural gas when you turn down the **Ⓒ** _____ .

details
You conserve electricity when you turn off **Ⓓ** _____ .
You can turn off toys and other things that run on **Ⓔ** _____ .

2. SUMMARIZE Use the chart to summarize this lesson.

3. VOCABULARY Use the word **conserve** to tell about this picture.

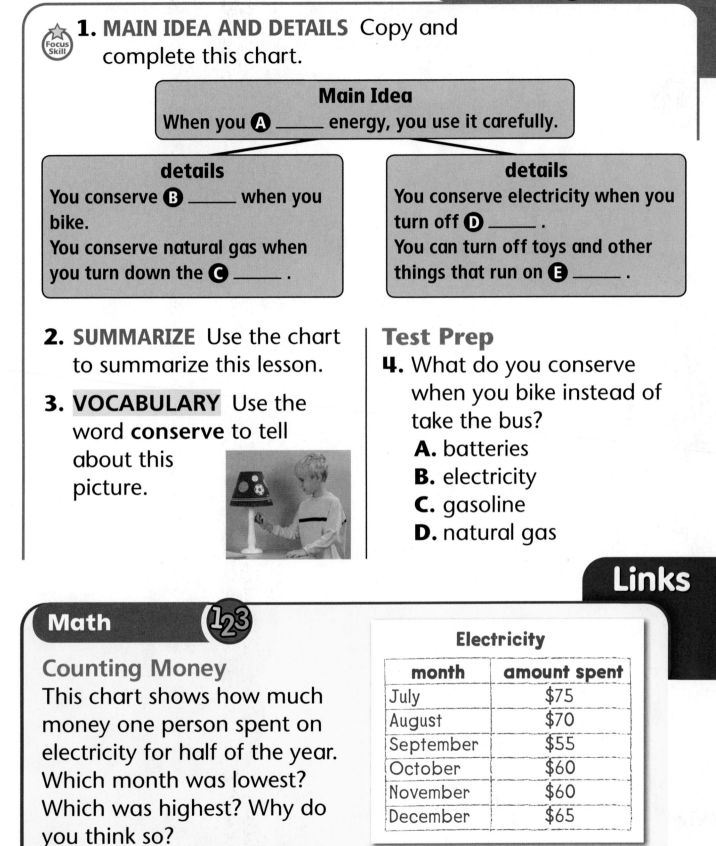

Test Prep

4. What do you conserve when you bike instead of take the bus?
   A. batteries
   B. electricity
   C. gasoline
   D. natural gas

Links

Math

Counting Money
This chart shows how much money one person spent on electricity for half of the year. Which month was lowest? Which was highest? Why do you think so?

Electricity	
month	amount spent
July	$75
August	$70
September	$55
October	$60
November	$60
December	$65

For more links and activities, go to www.hspscience.com

Where Do People Get Energy?

How You Use Energy

You need

- pencil
- paper

Step 1

Observe all the ways you use energy in one day. Make a list of things you do.

Step 2

In your list, circle the things that needed more energy.

Step 3

When did you need more energy? When did you need less? Explain what you observed.

Inquiry Skill

When you observe yourself, you are paying attention to what you do.

 PS-9 Describe energy sources, **SI-8** Communicate work, **SK-2** Demonstrate good explanations

251

VOCABULARY
food group

 READING FOCUS SKILL

CAUSE AND EFFECT Look for ways that energy from food helps you.

Energy from Food

People need food for energy. You need energy to move, play, and think. Energy helps you do all the things that you do each day.

Energy from food helps your body grow and stay healthy. Eating healthful food makes your body strong. It also helps keep your body from getting sick.

CAUSE AND EFFECT What can you do because you have energy?

Insta-Lab

Act It Out

How does it feel to have energy? Act this out. Then act out how it feels not to have energy. Why is it important to have energy to do things? Talk about it with a partner.

How are these children using energy?

Healthful Foods

A **food group** is one kind of food that you need to eat to stay healthy. Your body needs food from each of these food groups.

⭐ **CAUSE AND EFFECT** How does eating foods from each food group help you?

▲ fruits

milk, yogurt, and cheese

▲ vegetables

◀ meat, poultry, fish, beans, eggs, and nuts

◀ bread, cereal, rice, and pasta

254

Focus Skill **1. CAUSE AND EFFECT** Copy and complete this chart.

Healthful Foods

cause   effects

Eating healthful foods
→ gives your body **Ⓐ** _____ to do things.
→ makes your body **Ⓑ** _____.
→ keeps your body from getting **Ⓒ** _____.

2. SUMMARIZE Write two sentences to tell what this lesson is about.

3. VOCABULARY Use the words **food group** to tell about this picture.

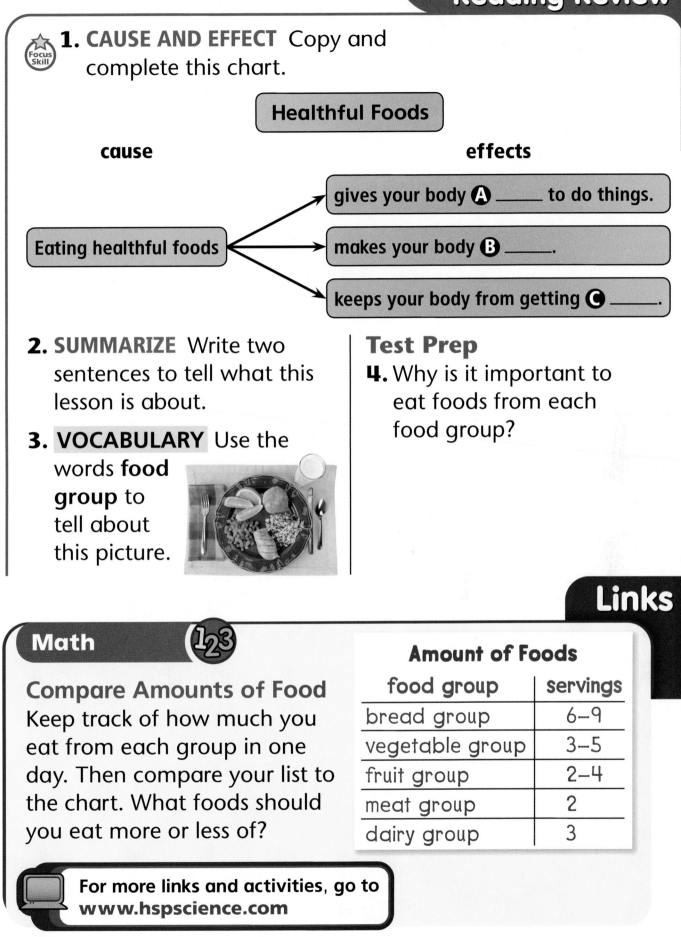

Test Prep

4. Why is it important to eat foods from each food group?

Links

Math 🄁🄂🄃

Compare Amounts of Food
Keep track of how much you eat from each group in one day. Then compare your list to the chart. What foods should you eat more or less of?

Amount of Foods

food group	servings
bread group	6–9
vegetable group	3–5
fruit group	2–4
meat group	2
dairy group	3

💻 **For more links and activities, go to www.hspscience.com**

How Cell Phones Work

Have you seen kids with cell phones? A cell phone is really a radio. It turns the sound of your voice into another kind of energy. This energy then travels through the air until it reaches a tower.

Dialing Out

The tower picks up the energy. Then the tower sends it out to the number you dialed.

The other person's phone turns the energy back into sound. Did you ever think you would be talking through the air?

THINK ABOUT IT

What does a cell phone do to your voice when you talk into it?

Find out more! Log on to
www.hspscience.com

Training for Success

Chi Lee likes to play table tennis. One year Chi decided to play in the Special Olympics!

A trainer helped Chi play better. He taught her how to hold the paddle. The trainer helped Chi choose foods that would give her lots of energy. "Good athletes work hard and eat healthful foods," said Chi. Chi hopes her hard work will help her win!

You Can Do It!

Materials
- small plant
- water
- foil

We Need the Sun

What to Do

1. Cover one leaf of the plant with foil.

2. Water the plant. Put it in a sunny place.

3. After three days, take the foil off the leaf. What happened to the leaf? Explain why.

Draw Conclusions

If you put a plant in a closet for a long time, what would happen? Why? Use this activity to help you explain your answer.

Plan a Healthful Meal

Cut out pictures of foods from old magazines. Choose one food from each healthful food group. Tape the foods to a paper plate to make a meal. Tell why your meal is healthful.

Review and Test Preparation

Vocabulary Review

Use the word or words to tell about the picture.

1. **energy** p. 236

2. **fuel** p. 239

3. **conserve** p. 246

4. **food group** p. 254

Check Understanding

5. Which **detail** tells one way you can conserve energy?

    A. Use batteries in your toys.

    B. Take a car to school.

    C. Turn the heat up.

    D. Turn off lights you do not need.

6. Where does most energy on Earth come from?

    F. heat

    G. light

    H. plants

    J. sun

Critical Thinking

7. Why do people sometimes need to get electricity from batteries?

8. Dana eats an apple. Explain how she is getting energy.

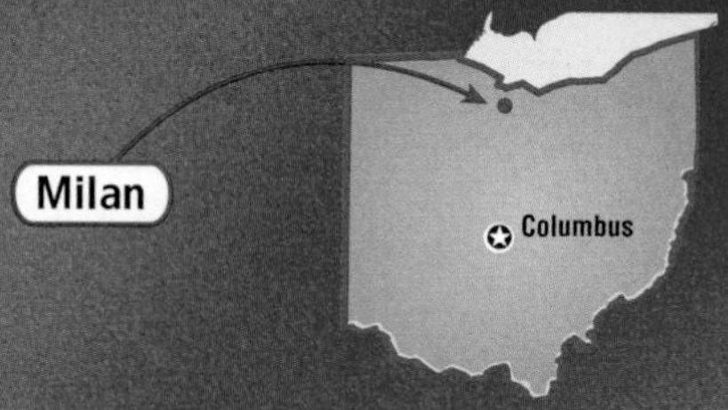

Milan

Columbus

Thomas Edison's Birthplace

Thomas Edison was an inventor. He was born in Milan, Ohio. His house is now a museum. You can find out about his life there.

Did you know that Thomas Edison invented the light bulb? He also made the movie camera!

phonograph

Thomas Edison was born here in 1847.

Edison's Favorite

Edison invented many things. He loved the phonograph best. It could play music loudly. That was important to him. He was almost deaf.

Thomas Edison experimenting with sound

Think and Do

1. **SCIENCE AND TECHNOLOGY** Draw a picture. Show how people cooked, lighted their homes, and kept warm before they had electricity. Why are inventions important?

2. **SCIENTIFIC THINKING** Look at the phonographs. What do you think the large cone-shaped object does? Try this to find the answer. Face your friends. First, say your name out loud. Next, say it through a paper-towel tube. Last, cover the end of the tube. Say your name again. What do your friends hear each time?

PS-5 Explore forces at a distance; **PS-6** Investigate changes in motion; **PS-7** Explore energy; **PS-9** Describe energy sources; **ST-2** Explain importance of following directions; **ST-7** Explore stages in building; **ST-8** Investigate how things work together

263

Huffman Prairie

Columbus

Huffman Prairie Flying Field

Orville and Wilbur Wright flew the first airplane in 1903. It stayed in the air only a few seconds.

They knew they could make a better airplane. They used a field near Dayton to experiment. They had room to fly their planes there.

the Wright brothers' first working airplane

UNIT C OHIO EXPEDITIONS

What did the Wright brothers do before they built airplanes? They worked in their bicycle shop.

They learned things about using gears. They also learned about forces and energy. Knowing these things helped them make an airplane.

Many other inventors have helped to make airplanes the way they are today.

the Wright Brothers

the Wright brothers' bicycle shop

The Wrights as Wheelmen

Think and Do

1. **SCIENCE AND TECHNOLOGY** Look at the photos. What bicycle parts did the Wright brothers use to build their airplanes? How did they know the airplanes would work?

2. **SCIENTIFIC THINKING** What kind of tools does it take to build an airplane? Do you think the Wright brothers could build an airplane without tools? Why or why not?

PS-6 Investigate changes in motion; **ST-2** Explain importance of following directions; **ST-6** Explore need for tools; **ST-7** Explore stages in building; **ST-8** Investigate how things work together

265

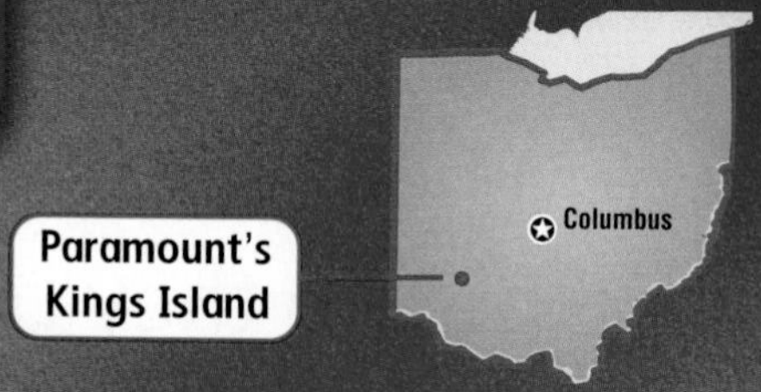

Paramount's
Kings Island

Columbus

The Grand Carousel

The Grand Carousel was built in 1926. It has 48 wooden horses. Each one was carved by hand. As the carousel turns, twenty of the horses stand still. They are called standers. The other 28 horses move up and down. They are called jumpers.

The Grand Carousel is part of Paramount's Kings Island.

Electricity makes the Grand Carousel turn. How did carousels move before electricity? At first, people pulled them. Then they used horses and mules to pull them. Later, carousels were built with a hand crank. Turning the crank made the gears turn. This made the carousel move.

The horses go round and round as the carousel turns.

Think and Do

I. **SCIENCE AND TECHNOLOGY** The wooden horses on the Grand Carousel were made by hand. How could you make an animal from wood? What tools would you use? Draw a picture of the animal you would make.

2. **SCIENTIFIC THINKING** Merry-go-rounds and carousels go around and around. Cut out magazine pictures of other things that move this way. Glue them to make a poster. What kind of force makes each one move?

PS-1 Classify objects by properties; **PS-6** Investigate changes in motion; **ST-1** Explain importance of following directions; **ST-6** Explore need for tools; **ST-7** Explore stages in building

267

Do You Hear What I Hear?

Edison had a special way of hearing at work. He put his phonograph on a wooden frame. When it played, he bit the frame. Why?

Materials
- tuning fork (or a regular fork)
- hard surface

What to Do
1. Strike the tuning fork on a table. Hold it near your ear, but don't touch your ear. Do you hear it hum?
2. Strike it again. Hold the end on the table. Does the humming sound louder?

Draw Conclusions
What happens when the tuning fork stops vibrating?

PS-3 Explore changes in properties; **PS-4** Explore physical and chemical changes; **ST-2** Explain importance of following directions; **ST-7** Explore stages in building; **ST-8** Investigate how things work together; **SK-1** Discover that experiments are repeatable

Flight Training

Materials
- sheets of paper
- paper clips
- instructions for folding a paper airplane

What to Do
1. Fold your paper to make an airplane. Fly it. Record how far it went.
2. Make a change to your airplane. Fly it. Record how far it went. Record whether it flew smoothly.
3. Change it again. Record how it flew.

Draw Conclusions
1. What made your plane fly its best?
2. Why was it good to have instructions to make your plane?

References

Contents

Your Senses

You have five senses that tell you about the world. Your five senses are sight, hearing, smell, taste, and touch.

Your Eyes

If you look at your eyes in a mirror, you will see an outer white part, a colored part called the iris, and a dark hole in the middle. This hole is called the pupil.

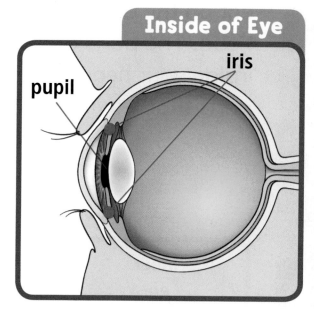

Inside of Eye

Caring for Your Eyes

- Have a doctor check your eyes to find out if they are healthy.

- Never look directly at the sun or at very bright lights.

- Wear sunglasses outdoors in bright sunlight and on snow and water.

- Don't touch or rub your eyes.

- Protect your eyes when you play sports.

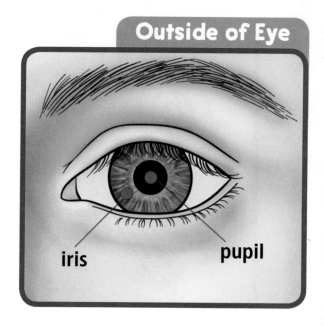

Outside of Eye

Your Senses

Your Ears

Your ears let you hear the things around you. You can see only a small part of the ear on the outside of your head. The parts of your ear inside your head are the parts that let you hear.

Caring for Your Ears

- Have a doctor check your ears.

- Avoid very loud noises.

- Never put anything in your ears.

- Protect your ears when you play sports.

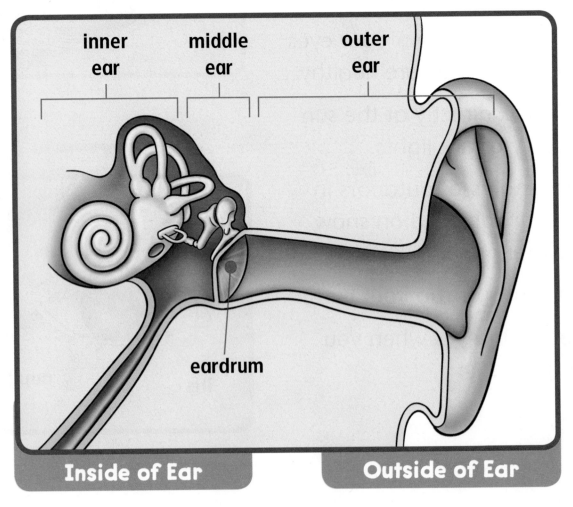

inner ear   middle ear   outer ear

eardrum

Inside of Ear   **Outside of Ear**

Your Senses of Smell and Taste

Your nose cleans the air you breathe and lets you smell things. Your nose and tongue help you taste things you eat and drink.

Your Skin

Your skin protects your body from germs. Your skin also gives you your sense of touch.

Caring for Your Skin

• Always wash your hands after coughing or blowing your nose, touching an animal, playing outside, or using the restroom.

• Protect your skin from sunburn. Wear a hat and clothes to cover your skin outdoors.

• Use sunscreen to protect your skin from the sun.

• Wear proper safety pads and a helmet when you play sports, ride a bike, or skate.

Your Skeletal System

Inside your body are many hard, strong bones. They form your skeletal system. The bones in your body protect parts inside your body.

Your skeletal system works with your muscular system to hold your body up and to give it shape.

Caring for Your Skeletal System

- Always wear a helmet and other safety gear when you skate, ride a bike or a scooter, or play sports.

- Eat foods that help keep your bones strong and hard.

- Exercise to help your bones stay strong and healthy.

- Get plenty of rest to help your bones grow.

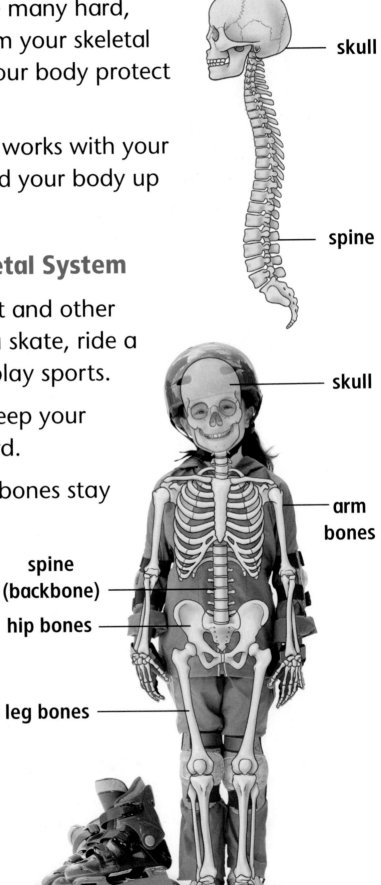

skull

spine

skull

arm bones

spine (backbone)

hip bones

leg bones

Your Muscular System

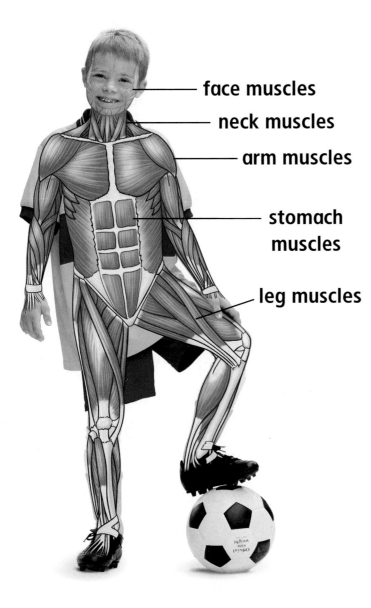

face muscles

neck muscles

arm muscles

stomach muscles

leg muscles

Your muscular system is made up of the muscles in your body. Muscles are body parts that help you move.

Caring for Your Muscular System

- Exercise to keep your muscles strong.

- Eat foods that will help your muscles grow.

- Drink plenty of water when you play sports or exercise.

- Rest your muscles after you exercise or play sports.

Your Nervous System

Your brain and your nerves are parts of your nervous system. Your brain keeps your body working. It tells you about the world around you. Your brain also lets you think, remember, and have feelings.

Caring for Your Nervous System

- Get plenty of sleep. Sleeping lets your brain rest.

- Always wear a helmet to protect your head and your brain when you ride a bike or play sports.

Your Digestive System

Your digestive system helps your body get energy from the foods you eat. Your body needs energy to do things.

When your body digests food, it breaks the food down. Your digestive system keeps the things your body needs. It also gets rid of the things your body does not need to keep.

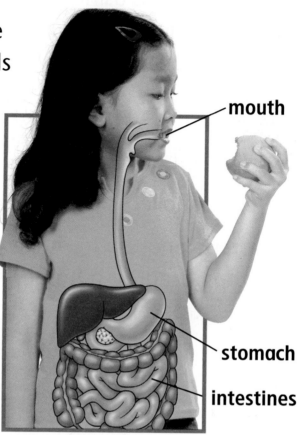

mouth

stomach

intestines

Caring for Your Digestive System

• Brush and floss your teeth every day.

• Wash your hands before you eat.

• Eat slowly and chew your food well before you swallow.

• Eat vegetables and fruits. They help move foods through your digestive system.

Your Respiratory System

You breathe using your respiratory system. Your mouth, nose, and lungs are all parts of your respiratory system.

Caring for Your Respiratory System

• Never put anything in your nose.

• Never smoke.

• Exercise enough to make you breathe harder. Breathing harder makes your lungs stronger.

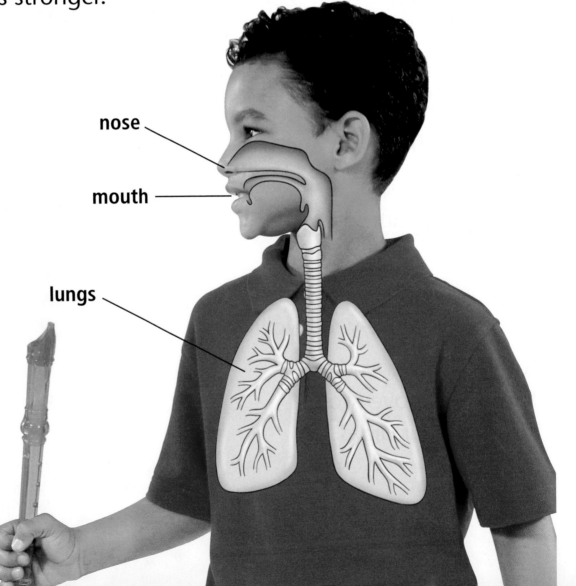

nose

mouth

lungs

Your Circulatory System

Your circulatory system is made up of your heart and your blood vessels. Your blood carries food energy and oxygen to help your body work. Blood vessels are small tubes. They carry blood from your heart to every part of your body.

Your heart is a muscle. It is beating all the time. As your heart beats, it pumps blood through your blood vessels.

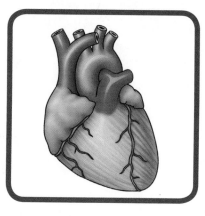

Caring for Your Circulatory System

• Exercise every day to keep your heart strong.

• Eat meats and green leafy vegetables. They help your blood carry oxygen.

• Never touch anyone else's blood.

R9

Staying Healthy

You can do many things to help yourself stay fit and healthy.

You can also avoid doing things that can harm you.

If you know ways to stay safe and healthy and you do these things, you can help yourself have good health.

Getting enough rest

Staying away from alcohol, tobacco, and other drugs

Staying active

Keeping clean

Eating right

Keeping Clean

Keeping clean helps you stay healthy. You can pick up germs from the things you touch. Washing with soap and water helps remove germs from your skin.

Wash your hands for as long as it takes to say your ABCs. Always wash your hands at these times.

• Before and after you eat

• After coughing or blowing your nose

• After using the restroom

• After touching an animal

• After playing outside

Caring for Your Teeth

Brushing your teeth and gums keeps them clean and healthy. You should brush your teeth at least twice a day. Brush in the morning. Brush before you go to bed at night. It is also good to brush your teeth after you eat if you can.

Brushing Your Teeth

Use a soft toothbrush that is the right size for you. Always use your own toothbrush. Use only a small amount of toothpaste. It should be about the size of a pea. Be sure to rinse your mouth with water after you brush your teeth.

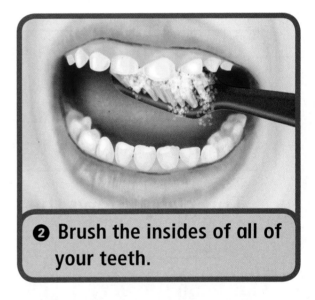

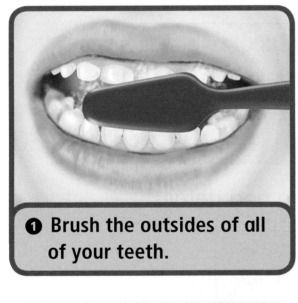

❶ Brush the outsides of all of your teeth.

❷ Brush the insides of all of your teeth.

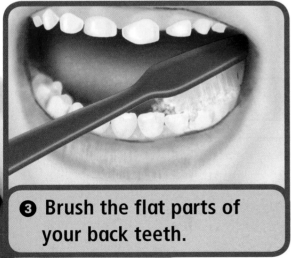

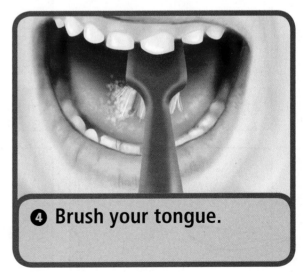

❸ Brush the flat parts of your back teeth.

❹ Brush your tongue.

Identify the Main Idea and Details

Some lessons in this science book are written to help you find the main idea. Learning how to find the main idea can help you understand what you read. The main idea of a paragraph is what it is mostly about. The details tell you more about it.

Read this paragraph.

Lions are hunters. They hunt for meat to eat. Lions can run very fast. They see and hear very well. They need sharp teeth to catch animals. They have sharp teeth to eat the meat they catch.

This chart shows the main idea and details.

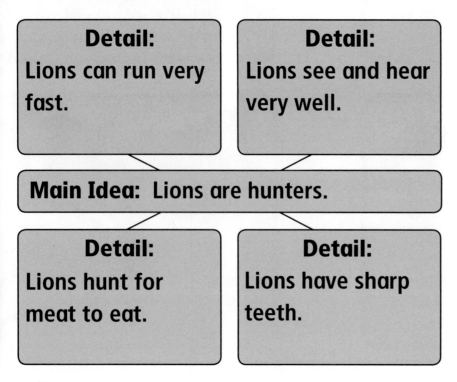

Detail:
Lions can run very fast.

Detail:
Lions see and hear very well.

Main Idea: Lions are hunters.

Detail:
Lions hunt for meat to eat.

Detail:
Lions have sharp teeth.

Compare and Contrast

Focus Skill

Some science lessons are written to help you see how things are alike and different. Learning how to compare and contrast can help you understand what you read.

Read this paragraph.

> Birds and mammals are kinds of animals. Birds have a body covering of feathers. Mammals have a body covering of fur. Both birds and mammals need food, air, and water to live. Most birds can fly. Most mammals walk or run.

Here is how you can compare and contrast birds and mammals.

Ways They Are Alike	Ways They Are Different
Compare	**Contrast**
Both are kinds of animals. Both need food, air, and water to live.	Birds have feathers. Mammals have fur. Most birds fly. Most mammals walk or run.

R15

Cause and Effect

Some science lessons are written to help you understand why things happen. You can use a chart like this to help you find cause and effect.

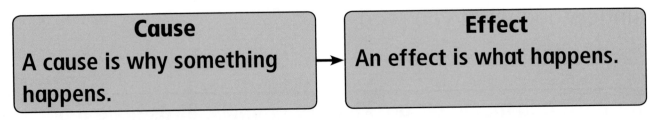

Cause	Effect
A cause is why something happens.	An effect is what happens.

Some paragraphs have more than one cause or effect. Read this paragraph.

Water can be a solid, a liquid, or a gas. When water is very cold, it turns into solid ice. When water is heated, it turns into water vapor, a gas.

This chart shows two causes and their effects in the paragraph.

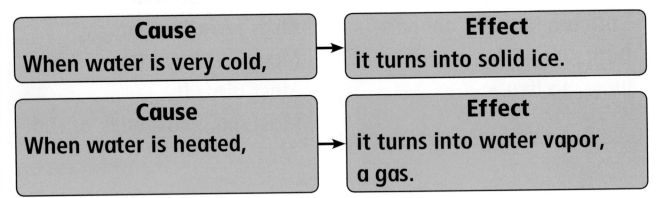

Cause	Effect
When water is very cold,	it turns into solid ice.

Cause	Effect
When water is heated,	it turns into water vapor, a gas.

Sequence

Learning how to find sequence can help you understand what you read. You can use a chart like this to help you find sequence.

| 1. The first step | → | 2. The next step | → | 3. The last step |

Some paragraphs use words that help you understand order. Read this paragraph. Look at the underlined words.

> Each day <u>begins</u> when the sun appears. <u>Then</u> the sun slowly climbs into the sky. At midday, the sun is straight overhead. <u>Then</u> the sun slowly falls back to the horizon. At <u>last</u>, the sun is gone. It is nighttime.

This chart shows the sequence of the paragraph.

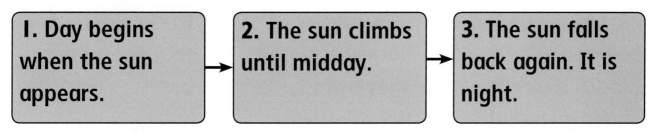

| 1. Day begins when the sun appears. | → | 2. The sun climbs until midday. | → | 3. The sun falls back again. It is night. |

At the end of some lessons, you will be asked to draw conclusions. When you draw conclusions, you tell what you have learned. What you learned also includes your own ideas.

Read this paragraph.

> Birds use their bills to help them get food. Each kind of bird has its own kind of bill. Birds that eat seeds have strong, short bills. Birds that eat bugs have long, sharp bills. Birds that eat water plants have wide, flat bills.

This chart shows how you can draw conclusions.

What I Read		**What I Know**		**Conclusion:**
Birds use their bills to get food. The bills have different shapes.	**+**	I have seen ducks up close. They have wide, flat bills.	**=**	Ducks are birds that eat water plants.

 Summarize

At the end of some lessons, you will be asked to summarize what you read. In a summary, some sentences tell the main idea. Some sentences tell details.

Read this paragraph.

> Honey is made by bees. They gather nectar from flowers. Then they fly home to their beehive with the nectar inside special honey stomachs. The bees put the nectar into special honeycomb holes. Then the bees wait. Soon the nectar will change into sweet, sticky honey. The bees cover the holes with wax that they make. They eat some of the honey during the cold winter.

This chart shows how to summarize what the paragraph is about.

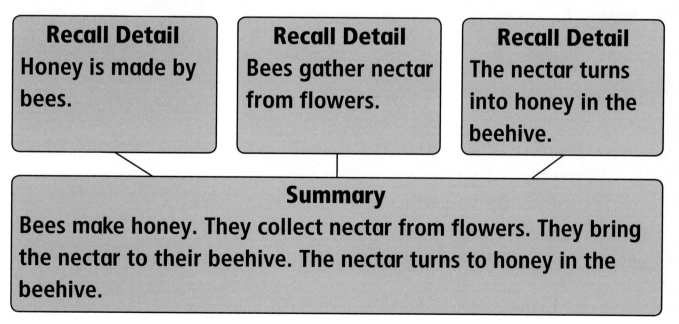

Recall Detail
Honey is made by bees.

Recall Detail
Bees gather nectar from flowers.

Recall Detail
The nectar turns into honey in the beehive.

Summary
Bees make honey. They collect nectar from flowers. They bring the nectar to their beehive. The nectar turns to honey in the beehive.

Using Tables, Charts, and Graphs

Gather Data

When you investigate in science, you need to collect data.

Suppose you want to find out what kinds of things are in soil. You can sort the things you find into groups.

Things I Found in One Cup of Soil

Parts of Plants

Small Rocks

Parts of Animals

By studying the circles, you can see the different items found in soil. However, you might display the data in a different way. For example, you could use a tally table.

Reading a Tally Table

You can show your data in a tally table.

Things I Found in ——— Title
One Cup of Soil

Items Found	Tally
Parts of Plants	ⲐⲐⲐⲐ Ⲓ
Parts of Animals	ⲒⲒⲒ
Small Rocks	ⲐⲐⲐⲐ ⲒⲒ

Tally marks

Data

How to Read a Tally Table

1. **Read** the tally table. Use the labels.

2. **Study** the data.

3. **Count** the tally marks.

4. **Draw conclusions**. Ask yourself questions like the ones on this page.

Skills Practice

1. How many parts of plants were found in the soil?

2. How many more small rocks were found in the soil than parts of animals?

3. How many parts of plants and parts of animals were found?

Using Tables, Charts, and Graphs

Reading a Bar Graph

People keep many kinds of animals as pets. This bar graph shows the animal groups pets belong to. A bar graph can be used to compare data.

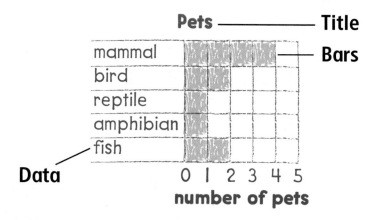

Pets —————— Title

mammal
bird
reptile
amphibian
fish

Bars

Data

0 1 2 3 4 5
number of pets

How to Read a Bar Graph

1. **Look** at the title to learn what kind of information is shown.

2. **Read** the graph. Use the labels.

3. **Study** the data. Compare the bars.

4. **Draw conclusions**. Ask yourself questions like the ones on this page.

Skills Practice

1. How many pets are mammals?

2. How many pets are birds?

3. How many more pets are mammals than fish?

Reading a Picture Graph

Members of a second-grade class were asked to choose their favorite season. A picture graph was made to show the results. A picture graph uses pictures to show information.

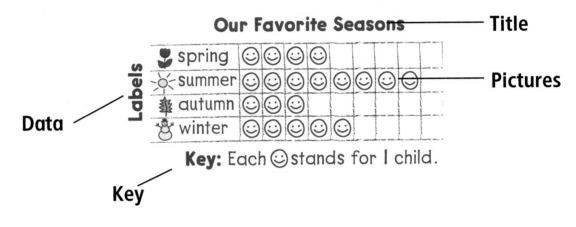

How to Read a Picture Graph

1. **Look** at the title to learn what kind of information is shown.

2. **Read** the graph. Use the labels.

3. **Study** the data. Compare the number of pictures in each row.

4. **Draw conclusions**. Ask yourself questions like the ones on this page.

Skills Practice

1. Which season did the most classmates choose?

2. Which season did the fewest classmates choose?

3. How many classmates in all chose summer or winter?

Measurements

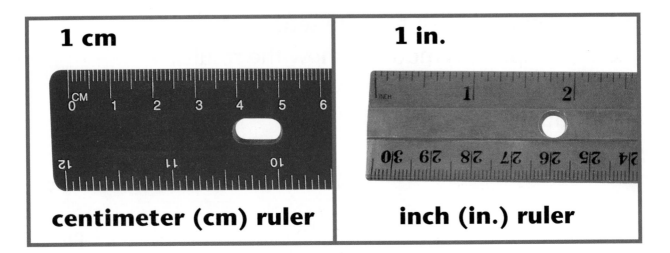

1 cm

CM 0 1 2 3 4 5 6

12 11 10

centimeter (cm) ruler

1 in.

INCH 1 2

24 25 26 27 28 29 30

inch (in.) ruler

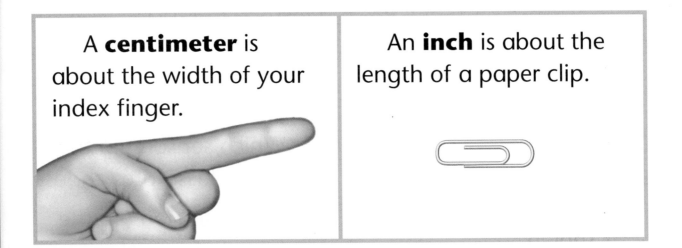

A **centimeter** is about the width of your index finger.

An **inch** is about the length of a paper clip.

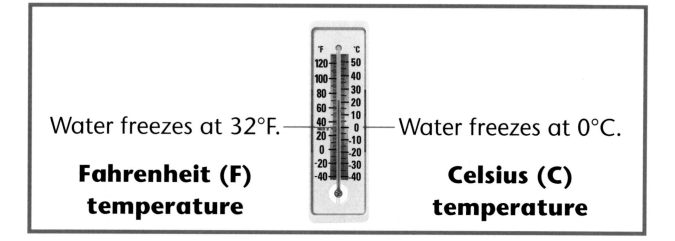

Water freezes at 32°F. — Water freezes at 0°C.

Fahrenheit (F) temperature　　　**Celsius (C) temperature**

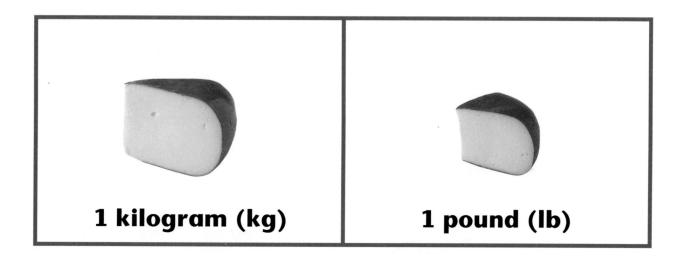

1 kilogram (kg)　　　**1 pound (lb)**

1 liter (L)　　　**1 cup (c)**

Safety in Science

Here are some safety rules to follow when you do activities.

1. **Think ahead.** Study the steps and follow them.

2. **Be neat and clean.** Wipe up spills right away.

3. **Watch your eyes.** Wear safety goggles when told to do so.

4. **Be careful with sharp things.**

5. **Do not eat or drink things.**

Glossary

A glossary lists words in alphabetical order. To find a word, look it up by its first letter or letters.

A

adaptation

A body part or behavior that helps a living thing. A horse has flat teeth to help it grind up its food. (96)

attract

To pull something. A magnet attracts things made of iron. (220)

B

burning

Changing of a substance into ashes and smoke. (186)

C

condensation

The change of water from a gas to a liquid. Condensation happens when heat is taken away from water vapor. (182)

R27

conserve

To use only what you need and not waste something. (246)

 **E**

electricity

A form of energy. People produce electricity by using energy from other sources. (240)

energy

Something that can cause matter to move or change. Heat, light, and sound are forms of energy. (236)

erosion

The carrying of rocks and soil to new places by moving water. Grass can help stop erosion. (48)

evaporation

The change of water from a liquid to a gas. Evaporation happens when heat is added to liquid water. (181)

F

fall

The season after summer, when the air begins to get cooler. (132)

food chain

A diagram that shows how animals and plants are linked by what they eat. (106)

food group

One kind of food that you need to eat to stay healthy. Vegetables are one of the food groups. (254)

force

Something that makes an object move or stop moving. (206)

fuel

Something that is burned for energy. Some fuels are gasoline, wood, coal, and oil. (239)

G

gills

The part of a fish that takes air from the water. (77)

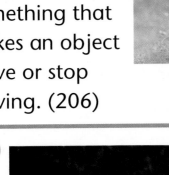

gravity

A force that pulls things down to the ground. (214)

H

heat

Energy that makes things warmer. Heat can be used to cook food or melt things. (236)

I

inquiry skills

The skills people use to find out information. (12)

L

light

A form of energy that lets you see. The sun and fires give off light energy. (237)

living

Needing food, water, and air to grow and change. (70)

lungs

The part of some animals that helps them breathe air. A pig has lungs. (77)

M

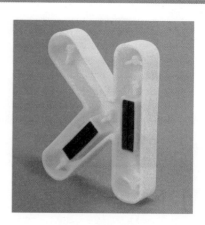

magnet

An object that will attract things made of iron. (220)

magnetic force

The pulling force of a magnet. (222)

mass

The measure of how much matter something has. You can measure mass with a balance. (164)

matter

Everything around you. Matter can be a solid, liquid, or gas. (162)

migrate

To move to a new place to find food. (134)

mixture

A mix of different kinds of matter. Substances in a mixture do not become other substances. (170)

motion

When something is moving. Jets are in motion when they move. (200)

natural resource

Anything from nature that people can use. (32)

nutrients

Minerals in the soil that plants need to grow and stay healthy. (84)

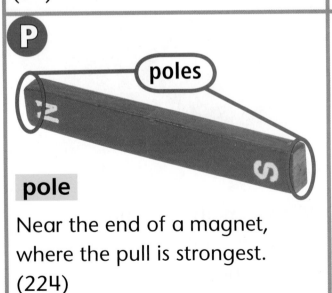

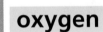

pole

Near the end of a magnet, where the pull is strongest. (224)

nonliving

Not needing food, water, and air and not growing. (71)

oxygen

A kind of gas that plants give off and animals need to breathe. (103)

pollen

A powder that flowers need to make seeds. (104)

pollution

Waste that causes harm to land, water, or air. (38)

property

One part of what something is like. Color, size, and shape are each a property. (164)

pull

To tug an object closer to you. (207)

push

To press an object away from you. (207)

R

recycle

To use old resources to make new things. (41)

reduce

To use less of a natural resource. (40)

repel

To push away. Poles that are the same on magnets repel each other. (224)

reuse

To use a natural resource again. (41)

S

science tools

The tools that help scientists find what they need. (20)

season

A time of year. A year has four seasons. The seasons are spring, summer, fall, and winter. (118)

senses

The way we tell what the world is like. The five senses are sight, hearing, smell, taste, and touch. (4)

shelter

A place where animals can be safe. (78)

speed

The measure of how fast something moves. (201)

spring

The season after winter, when the weather gets warmer. (120)

summer

The season after spring, which is usually hot. Summer has many hours of daylight. (126)

sunlight

Light that comes from the sun. (83)

W

water vapor

Water that is in the form of a gas. (181)

winter

The season after fall, which is usually cold. Winter has the fewest hours of daylight. (138)

Index

R38

Photography Credits

SELF-PROTECTION An arctic fox curls up in the snow. Then it covers its nose and face with its tail.

YOUNG An arctic fox gives birth to 4-11 pups at a time.

BEHAVIOR The arctic fox stores food during the summer.

CAMOUFLAGE The arctic fox has fur that changes color with the season.

SELF-PROTECTION Thick fur keeps an arctic fox's feet warm.